Advance Praise for
Welcome to Pawnee

"Filled with hilarious stories and sweet obser-
vations, *Welcome to Pawnee* is a book for any *Parks and Rec* fan. It's
funny and straight from the heart, and it took me back to the absolute
joy it was to make this show with people like our dear Jim O'Heir. Jim
did a great job of not Jerry-ing this book."

—Amy Poehler

"It pains me to say anything nice about this undeniably
charming book from the actor who played Jerry Gergich. So I won't.
I mean, sure, you could chuckle at these delightful showbiz stories
or have your heart strings tugged by the various hijinks of the *Parks
and Rec* cast. OR, you could watch season 7, episode 8 of *The New
Yankee Workshop* with Norm Abram on how to build a wooden Clancy
boat—a handsome ten-foot sailing dinghy that will provide many more
hours of fun than some dumb actor book."

—Nick Offerman

"So anyone who's ever heard me talk about Jim O'Heir
knows he's my favorite. He's thoughtful, generous, and occasionally
funny . . . occasionally. So when he asked me to read this and give a
quote, I charged him the friends-and-family rate. You know, because
friendship. But I'm happy to report that I enjoyed this damn thing.
Especially since I didn't think he was a great speller. The stories take
me back to our *Parks and Rec* days and give me the warm fuzzies.
You may not feel nostalgic ('cause you weren't there), but you will get
an idea of what a truly singular experience being on *Parks and Recreation* was."

—Retta

"There is no one more qualified to write the definitive *Parks and Rec* book than the unbelievably hilarious, one-of-a-kind talent we all know and love: Tim—I mean Jim—O'Heir."

—Adam Scott

"This book is full of lies. Only the Dark Lord himself knows the truth about Pawnee. Do not trust Jerry."

—~~Aubrey Plaza~~ April Ludgate

"I vividly remember the very first time I ever spoke to Jim O'Heir. It was season 5's wrap party. Since then I've been a fan. I'm super excited to have my assistant read and tell me about this book!"

—Rob Lowe

"So glad Jim has written this book and now it's my duty to urge you to 'treat yourself' and your bookshelf to this wonderful memoir."

—Aziz Ansari

"Not even Ben Wyatt or Barney Varmn could have put together such a masterful account of the making of the show. Excited to dig in and enjoy the $25 Jim paid me for this blurb."

—Greg Levine

"Damn it, O'Heir! You've written one of the best, most heart-felt reminiscences of one of the best shows to ever be on TV!"

—Patton Oswalt

"Jim's writing is like an old friend telling the best stories I always wanted to hear but never had access to. In other words, he KA-BOOMed it!"

—Paul Scheer

Welcome to Pawnee

Welcome to

WHEN YOU'RE HERE, THEN YOU'RE HOME

WM

WILLIAM MORROW

An Imprint of HarperCollinsPublishers

Pawnee

Stories of Friendship, Waffles, and *Parks and Recreation*

JIM O'HEIR

HarperCollins books may be purchased for educational, business, or sales promotional use. For information, please email the Special Markets Department at SPsales@harpercollins.com.

FIRST EDITION

Designed by Bonni Leon-Berman

Library of Congress Cataloging-in-Publication Data
Names: O'Heir, Jim, 1962- author.
Title: Welcome to Pawnee : stories of friendship, waffles, and Parks and recreation / Jim O'Heir.
Description: First edition. | New York : William Morrow, an imprint of HarperCollins Publishers, 2024.
Identifiers: LCCN 2024024214 | ISBN 9780063293502 (hardcover) | ISBN 9780063293526 (ebook)
Subjects: LCSH: Parks and recreation (Television program)
Classification: LCC PN1992.77.P2655 O34 2024 | DDC 791.45/72–dc23/eng/20240607
LC record available at https://lccn.loc.gov/2024024214

ISBN 978-0-06-329350-2

24 25 26 27 28   TC   10 9 8 7 6 5 4 3 2 1

I dedicate this book to you.
No, not you . . .
THE PLURAL YOU!

For the fans of
Parks and Recreation.
Your love for Pawnee,
waffles, and
Li'l Sebastian
has never wavered.

Contents

Welcome to Pawnee

Boola Boola Boola!

This was a good day. A great day.
One of the best. I got to pee standing up.

We're ambling through the sun-dappled forest when—

Bang!

Nick Offerman is shot.

Wait! We're on set. That's Ron Swanson, not Nick Offerman.

We're filming "Hunting Trip," the tenth episode of the second season of *Parks and Recreation*—the show that would come to define my career as well as introduce me to lifelong friends—and we're on location, far from the soundstage. This is why we find ourselves in the Angeles National Forest when poor old Ron is struck in the back of the head by a stray bullet.

Since you're already a big *Parks* fan, you know Tom Haverford shot Ron Swanson.

Jerry wasn't yet established as a series regular, so imagine my surprise when I pored over the script prior to that week's table read and came to the part where Jerry looks square into the camera, grabs a beer, and says, "This is such a great day. See, at my house, I've got a wife and three beautiful daughters. But this trip, it is the one time of year I get to pee standing up."

That line from my "talking head" segment (when a character directly addresses the camera) was a turning point for my role. It signaled that the writers and producers cared enough about Jerry to create a backstory, and it suggested I had a future with the show, even if I wasn't sure of the specifics, including the eventual story arc that I was married to a character played by a certain supermodel.

My pal Retta also had some good news by way of her character. Shortly after Ron is shot, causing panic and turmoil in an already anxiety-fueled episode, a secondary scream is heard, this time from Donna Meagle. Ann Perkins, a selfless nurse, believes that Donna is having a heart attack, with good reason, until it becomes clear that Donna is hyperventilating because someone has shot at her prized Mercedes. It's apparent that the lady likes nice things, a trait that comes full circle in season 4's "Pawnee Rangers," aka "Treat. Yo. Self."

We all grew much closer on that trip. I remember Retta walking backward up a hill to alleviate pressure on her bad knees as we guided her to make sure she didn't veer off the road. There were Paul Schneider and I, chopping it up and telling each other dirty jokes till we went blue,[*] or Amy Poehler and I, screaming unintelligible chants as we ran through the trees—*Boola boola boola!* There were besties Amy and Rashida Jones laughing so hard that they could barely make it through a scene, which happened often and at random—in this episode, it's when they force an angry Ron Swanson back to his bed so that he can convalesce. They repeatedly cry-laughed, "Nick is so strong! How is he this strong?"

Amy recovered in time for Leslie to give her alibis to the ranger at the end of the episode, when she realizes she's dealing with a misogynistic A-hole. If you want to watch a master class in improv comedy, check this out again. Here are a few of my favorite lines, most of which were made up by Amy on the spot: "I was thinking with my lady parts"; "I'm wearing a new bra and it closes in the front and it popped open and it threw me off"; "Bitches be crazy"; "I'm good at tolerating pain. Bad at math. And stupid." In my opinion, Leslie finds her character-footing in "Hunting Trip." She's smart, zany, and uncompromising.

And for me? This episode provided me with a boost in confidence, the most I'd felt since joining the cast. After all, this had

---

[*] If there's an unrated version of *Welcome to Pawnee*, rest assured I will include them.

been a new show by the great Greg Daniels and the precocious Michael Schur, a Harvard graduate and Greg's partner in crime. In addition to being the creator and showrunner for the American version of *The Office*, Greg cocreated *King of the Hill* and was a writer on shows such as *Saturday Night Live* and *The Simpsons*. Michael was also an *SNL* alum, the writer and producer of its popular Weekend Update segment. He'd go on to cocreate *The Good Place*, *Brooklyn Nine-Nine*, and *Master of None*. No small feat. If these stalwarts weren't proof enough, *Parks and Recreation* starred elite *SNL* alum and improv queen Amy Poehler and was pitched as NBC's next big investment. Was I nervous? No. I was absolutely terrified.

Which is funny all these years later when people yell to me on the street, "*Hey, it's Jerry/Larry/Terry/Garry/Barry!*" Or when I'm stopped in a café and asked if "Pawnee's mayor" wouldn't mind taking a photo. Of course I don't mind—anything for my citizens.

After appearing on seven seasons of the show, and on every episode no less, I want to put on my hunting cap, zip up that old fleece-lined vest, and walk you through the years of *Parks*, with all the silliness, joyful moments, and crazy good fortune of making art with my friends. Friends who enjoy catching you with your pants down. You remember the episode, don't you?

I can still hear Retta's delirious laughter after watching Aziz getting pantsed by Amy. "Ohhhh, Aziz be packing!" Retta cried. Unfortunately, that never made the final cut.

I even got pantsed, though not by the "Pants Queen," Leslie. That honor was done by Mark Brendanawicz. If that doesn't make you one of the team, I don't know what does.

The Incredibly Long-Winded and Exhaustively Untitled TV Project

Word was going 'round about the Untitled Greg Daniels and Michael Schur Project, which seemed a little wordy, which is why it was mostly called the Untitled Amy Poehler Project (tie goes to the alliteration). If you've been around showbiz as long as I have, you learn of these types of projects as if they're gossip bombs dropped in middle school hallways. I couldn't go into any audition in those days without overhearing an actor mentioning how badly they wanted in on it.

Did you hear Greg and Mike are doing an Office *spin-off?*

Did you hear Amy Poehler is headlining a new thing by Greg and Mike from The Office*?*

That's TV royalty, man. It's gonna be so good; you gotta get an audition. You gotta call your manager!

So I did. I called my manager, Lynda, who confirmed the rumor and told me she'd try to get me in on it.

Amy, coming off her sterling work on *SNL*, was the project's champion, which meant that any auditions would be super competitive and nearly impossible to get into. Imagine it: *The Office*, created by Daniels, had hit its peak in 2008, at the time this "new project" was making its way through Hollywood.

Greg Daniels, *Cocreator*

Between season 2 and season 3 of *The Office*, we left Jim [Halpert] on this note of, "If he doesn't get Pam, then he can't stay on the show." And I think everyone in the audience assumed that we'd figure some way around that, but then we started season 3 and he moved to Stamford, Connecticut, where he was at another branch of Dunder Mifflin. So, to create this other branch, we had to cast this satellite version of the office. We had Ed Helms, Rashida [Jones], and some others as well. At that point, Ben Silverman, who was the guy who got the rights to *The Office* and who brought me on to adapt it, was now president of NBC. He saw the Stamford branch and said, "You need to spin off *The Office*. Look at how you were able to create this whole other thing, and, you know, I wouldn't mind watching a show called *The Stamford Branch*."

I was reluctant because the idea of a spin-off felt like a throwback to an era of television that was . . . I don't know . . . I thought it was going to hurt the original show. I thought it would zap some of the energy. I kept putting it off, but [Ben] was insistent. So I started to think about how this could work.

I had two ideas for writers who could leave *The Office* for this idea, and one of them was Mike [Schur], who's extremely self-assured and capable. The other was [writer and showrunner] Jen Celotta. I started meeting with Mike before work at a place called Norms Restaurant, and we were coming up with different ideas. I was very into this 1970s documentary called *An American Family*, about the Loud family, and it was not on air. I managed to find it in, like, a museum. I thought the mockumentary format could work well. I felt like that would be the best idea for a spin-off, but we had other ideas.

One of the ideas was, "If *The Office* is about private industry, let's do something about the public sector. And maybe they'll be different enough—a government story versus a business story." Remember, one of my fears about doing *The Stamford Branch* was that the two shows would cannibalize each other. Mike preferred this other idea.

I also didn't want to leave people like Steve Carell in the lurch, to make it seem like I wasn't coming back. That wouldn't work. So I thought I could set it up where Mike could run *Parks*. I had this other idea for a family and thought Jen Celotta could run that. About a family on a cul-de-sac, starring Catherine Tate. I love her.

Anyway, we're building the concept for *Parks*, and one of the things we didn't want to have was a male lead. We didn't want to do the same stuff as *The Office*. We were a little scared based on the enthusiasm from the network, scared that they would do some forced crossover thing between the two shows. So, we decided we didn't want it to be a traditional spin-off. Part of spiking that tire was having Rashida Jones being on the show but being a different person—you can't spin off that.

Mike said, "What about Amy Poehler?" I thought that was fantastic. Of all the people of that generation from Second City—Steve Carell, Stephen Colbert, Amy Sedaris, and Tina Fey, they were all birthed out of the same Chicago scene. Bob Odenkirk, too. Part of the challenge of making a show is: how do you find someone who has all the chops and comedy experience but who hasn't been discovered yet? Amy was super popular but hadn't done her own thing yet. We had been so lucky getting Steve Carell for *The Office* because he had all the juice of a star like Will Ferrell, but he hadn't been a movie star yet. I had this feeling with Amy like, "Yes, she's coming off *SNL* and maybe she has a higher profile than Steve Carell, who did *The Daily Show*, but it was sketch comedy. It was a different thing."

The first actor we hired was Aziz Ansari, though. I was a huge fan of this sketch that he wrote on a show called *Human Giant*, the one where this guy gets views on YouTube by cutting his own penis off. But Aziz gets views by making silly faces, and he gets slightly more views. That was one of the funniest things I ever saw. I did some research and learned that Aziz wrote that sketch, and I thought, *This is perfect. A writer-performer.* One of the first people we hired on *The Office* was B. J. [Novak], and I originally thought that Aziz would be in the writers' room, but anyway . . .

We got Amy. And there wasn't going to be a pilot for this show; it was straight to TV. Ben was my buddy and he needed something fast, and he had also done *The Office*, which was the number one show at the time. There is a drawback to this, though, in that you can't work out the kinks too much.

Show cocreator Mike Schur and Amy Poehler, the dream team.

Mike Schur, *Cocreator*

Amy got pregnant and she was supposed to give birth basically the week we started shooting. At the time, NBC had given us a post–Super Bowl slot. We were going to air after the Super Bowl. It was going to be *The Office* after the Super Bowl and then the *Parks* pilot after *The Office*. It wasn't an actual post–Super Bowl slot, but 28 million people or whatever were going to watch the show. We talked to Amy early on and then she was like, "I think I'm out." I don't think we even had an idea when we talked to her. We might have had the earliest germ of an idea, but it was like, "We can't do it with her; that's too bad."

Once we started really developing the show and built it around a woman who was the main character, we started to have this feeling . . . I remember this conversation we had where I was like, "I have worked with Amy. I know who she is and what she is capable of. There is no one else who can do this. We could have Allison Jones go out and find other actors, but this is just Amy Poehler; it just has to be." So we went back to Amy and said, "If we can wait for you and change your schedule, would you do it?" She said yes. We went back to NBC and said, "Listen, we are going to voluntarily give up the post–Super Bowl slot in order to get Amy Poehler." Our thinking was that the Super Bowl slot is a short-term decision; that's a decision you make to be explosive and firework-y and get as many people to see the pilot as you can, but getting Amy Poehler in your show is a long-term decision. It's the thing that's going to make the show work.

We had been guaranteed thirteen episodes on the air in the first season, and our pilot was going to air after the Super Bowl. I think we are the only people in history to voluntarily cut our order from thirteen to six and give up a Super Bowl slot, and it was purely to get Amy to do the show.

She gave birth and then, like, heroically, within three months after giving birth, she was on our set shooting the pilot. I am happy to say, all of these years later, that we made the right call. That show doesn't work if Amy is not at the center of it.

I learned that the well-regarded and brilliant Allison Jones, casting director for shows such as *The Fresh Prince of Bel-Air*, *Curb Your Enthusiasm*, *Arrested Development*, and many more, would be spearheading the casting process. This gave the project even more clout. Greg Daniels, Michael Schur, Amy Poehler, and now Allison Jones?

From the start, the project was fueled by rumors based upon the "breakdown" offered by Breakdown Services Ltd., a site that releases casting notices for TV and film. These casting notices go to agents and managers, which then filter down to actors. Since Greg Daniels's and Amy Poehler's names were attached to this breakdown, along with a logline about a mockumentary style, many assumed that the project would be too similar in tone and format to *The Office*, which was famous for its mockumentary, single-camera format. If that was true, then it was also fine with me. For one thing, I'm a huge fan of *The Office* and the show's lead, Steve Carell. I knew Steve from my Chicago days, and we had even done a voiceover job together for some beer campaign before I moved to Los Angeles. Getting to join something that would, in the worst case, copy the formula of *The Office* or, in the best, echo it would be a dream come true.

When word got out that Rashida Jones (no relation to Allison), who was a fixture of *The Office*'s seasons 3 and 4 and a key interloper in the relationship between Pam and Jim, would also be involved, the naysayers complained, "Now it really is *The Office*." *Oh well, let them complain*, I thought. *I still want in.*

Mike Schur

When we started to form the idea, we knew Aziz from his work on *Human Giant* and we were like, I don't know what role that guy is going to play, but that guy is funny; let's get that guy on the show. Aziz signed on to the show without having even heard the idea. Then, there was Rashida—I've known Rashida since the second day of college, but Rashida had been on *The Office*, playing Karen. It was like, "Rashida, come on board," and she was like, "Great." We had Rashida and Aziz, at least, having committed to the show before we really knew what the show was, if memory serves.

Greg was very wary of breaking up the kind of magic formula of *The Office*, and he had long believed that the key to that show's success was how many different characters there were. He used to tell us that we will know that the show is a success when people start coming up and saying, "My favorite character is Stanley," or "My favorite character is Phyllis," or "My favorite character is Kelly," or you know. Even though there were so many people in the show, he was very concerned about the idea of moving some of the actors into a different show. So, what he said to me was, "Look, they want this spin-off, but I told them I was just going to kind of do my best to come up with a good idea, and if that idea happens to be a spin-off, then great. And if it doesn't, we will do something else." So he asked me if I wanted to do it with him, which was amazing, and we spent a long time thinking of a bunch of different ideas. We thought about spin-offs of *The Office* with different characters; we thought about new ideas; we thought about family shows, work shows, whatever.

Eventually we got to this point where we had this idea,

which was basically that there is a woman who works in government, and there is a giant pit in a lot and she wants to turn it into a park. We really liked that as the starting point. And the thing that we liked about it the most was that with *The Office*, Greg Daniels, Ricky Gervais, and Stephen Merchant had done what amounted to a satire of all of corporate culture. And they did it by just picking this tiny kind of unimportant office in this unimportant industry in this unimportant part of the country and then examining what it's like to work in that office, and really, in any office anywhere. It was so relatable because everybody has worked in an office—it was like everyone has had a crush on someone they worked with, everyone has had an annoying boss, whatever.

We realized that by doing this idea, we had the chance to do for an entire town what *The Office* did for a work environment. Everyone has lived in a town, so everyone knows about the park system, the local celebrity journalist Joan Callamezzo–type person, the mayor, the parks where you played soccer when you were a kid, and the public swimming pool. We realized we could create an entire fictional city in the way that Greg, Ricky, and Stephen had created a fictional company, and that started to get interesting to us because it's really about world building. If we do this right, and the show lasts a long time, we will get to this point where Pawnee is a real place—it has rich history, and it has all sorts of people who live in it, who can float in and out like in *The Simpsons*.

We settled on that idea, and I think NBC still would have preferred, honestly at the time, that it be a spin-off, because spin-offs at the time were very valuable things. But Greg, true to his word, was like, "We are going to pick the best idea, and the best idea is the one we will write."

Greg Levine, *Script Coordinator and My Cohost on the* Parks and Recollection *Podcast*

I lost my job during the 2007–08 writers' strike. I had a buddy working as Allison Jones's casting assistant when he called to say, "Come over here, we need a second set of hands around the office, just answering phones and whatnot." I had no interest in casting, but Allison hired me sight unseen. Little did I know it then, but she would end up being one of the nicest people I've ever met.

Anyway, we cast *The Office* that season and it was soon revealed that *The Office* was going to do a spin-off that was probably going to be about Dwight. Unbeknownst to me, about once a week, Allison Jones called Greg Daniels to tell him that he should hire me to be their writers' assistant. One day we went to the *Office* set for season 4, and Allison pulls me over and asks if I want to meet Greg. I talk to Greg for a minute or two and then he asks if I want to meet any of the writers. I'm thinking, *What?! What have I stepped into? This is so cool.* We walk through the set to an office where Mike Schur and Jen Celotta are, and I start shooting the shit with Mike. We talked about *The West Wing* and *M*A*S*H* for five minutes, shows we both loved, when he

Writer extraordinaire Dan Goor and me goofing off.

told me about this new show they were launching and asked me if I wanted to come on as a writers' assistant. That's when I realized that that's the way you should interview—you should interview when you're not realizing you're interviewing. And that's how I ended up being there, the first person hired on *Parks and Recreation*. I was there pilot to finale.

On the set of Hot in Cleveland.
This is one group of funny ladies, led by queen-of-funny Betty White.

I had grown up loving shows featuring ensemble casts: *M*A*S*H*, *Cheers*, *Mary Tyler Moore*, *All in the Family*, *The Dick Van Dyke Show*, and heck, *The Golden Girls* (RIP to my girl Betty White), where a main character could recede at any time in service of another cast member's story. *The Office* harkened back to the time of Golden Age TV—full of quick dialogue, tight plotting, and surprising character arcs. The only drawback I imagined was there'd be no part for me.

I had reason to think this: a few years earlier, I'd auditioned for Allison Jones for a guest spot on *The Office* and didn't get it. If I'd failed to make the cut for a show like this one in the past, then why would I succeed now? I leapt from grief's first stage to the last, simply accepting I wouldn't be part of it.

You can imagine my delight when my manager, Lynda Bensky, called and told me I'd been invited to come in. "Don't mess it up," she said.* I arrived at the audition to find a bunch of macho men with big chests and strong jawlines. Why? I was auditioning for the role of Ron Swanson.

You and I both know there could only be one Ron Swanson, and his name is Nick Offerman. If you talk to Nick in real life, you can see Ron Swanson's characteristics at play: the monotone, the fascination with

This, my friends, is not a test. It's a selfie by one of the most selfless people I've ever known, Mr. Nick Swanson. I mean, Ron Offerman.

woodworking and other trades, the mustache . . . the mustache! Nick influenced the development of Ron Swanson as much as Ron Swanson reflected some of Nick's nature, and it was a perfect marriage of actor and character.

Mike Schur and Me

MIKE: I wrote an episode of *The Office* and the idea behind the episode was that Michael Scott goes to New York City,

---

* Lynda, in fact, is a lovely woman and would've never said this, but I like to pretend she's a tough-as-nails ball breaker. Sorry, Lynda.

and there is a meeting at the corporate offices with all of the managers of the regional branches. Michael managed the Scranton branch, and then there was the Buffalo branch and the Albany branch and the Stamford, Connecticut, branch and whatever. The reason we wanted to do this episode was there was a feeling, an earned feeling, which was basically like, "How does this idiot have a job?" Right?

ME: Yes, I love *The Office* and I say it every day. "How does the idiot have a job?"

MIKE: The guy is a moron. How does he have his job? So, the idea was, we are going to go to this meeting with all of the regional managers, and we are going to show you that in the corporate world, any idiot can be a regional manager. He had done absolutely nothing at all to prepare. The idea was that Michael Scott might be an idiot and a moron, but when push comes to shove, he also does the thing he is supposed to do. Whereas there is this guy in this other branch and that guy is a total moron.

The guy who played the part is named Craig Anton, and he is very funny. But when we first were auditioning people for the role, Nick Offerman came in. I lost my mind. He was so funny and weird. I remember him leaving after the audition and it being very clear that he was the right guy. I said to Allison, "How is that guy forty years old and I've never heard of him before, never seen him before? How does a person that good at comedy and acting get to be that age without any of us having had any idea who he is?" It turned out that he had had this kind of wild history of getting cast in pilots and then getting recast after table reads because he was too weird or whatever. He had just kind of managed to kind of fall through the cracks. So, we offered him the job, and I was so excited . . . and he said no. The reason he said no was because he had a guest spot already booked that week on *Will & Grace*.

ME: Where Megan was . . .

MIKE: I said he should bail on them; there won't be a better part than this. This is a juicy part, and he was like, "No, I'm married to Megan Mullally." I was like, "Fair enough. Go do your wife's show." I wrote down the name Nick Offerman on a Post-it note and put it on my computer. I left it there because I thought, *Someday there will be another part and that guy is going to be right for the part.*

Years went by and then this role came up, and I was like, "That's the guy. It's Nick Offerman!" I talked to Allison Jones and said, "This is Nick Offerman's part; let's just get him in here and read him." Greg, true to his word and character, said we should read a bunch of people. So, Allison brought in a bunch of people, and one of those people was Mike O'Malley. Mike came in before Nick and just blew the doors off the place with his audition. He was so great, and suddenly it was like, "Oh no, what do I do?" I was suddenly terrified because there was this other great performance. Then Nick came in and he was great, and I was even more tortured and whatever. Eventually it got to the point where we had these discussions, and it was like, "You know what, our gut was Nick; Nick was the guy. We kind of had him in our brain, and let's go with him."

I remember I wrote Mike an email. I was like, "Listen, man, I don't know if this will make you feel better or worse, but you gave as good an audition as you could give. You were perfect. There is nothing that you did that wasn't great. It's just that I had this guy's name on a Post-it note on my computer for three years, and I kind of just think that that's the way we are going to go." He wrote me back the nicest note that said, "Hey, man, the show is great. Nick Offerman is great. It's going to be awesome. No hard feelings." What a good guy. I am still friends with him, very good friends with him, now.

To me, that was the universe saying everything was going to be okay. The truth is that there is a tremendous amount of good fortune that plays into any project like this one lasting for a long time and being successful, but it's also not so much a miracle as it is just a lot of good people doing a lot of good work. There is an aspect of miracle, luck, good fortune, whatever, but there's another aspect of the best casting director in the world and the best TV producer in the world working together and finding one of the best actors in the world. When you think of it that way, it's less fragile, I think, then sometimes I feel like it was.

ME: Had Nick done the guest spot on *The Office*, would that have negated his possible role?

MIKE: Totally possible. Who knows? That's what is funny. I think he would have been great. Rashida, obviously, had been on *The Office* for a whole year, and we cast her. I'm not saying we wouldn't have cast him for that reason, but everything kind of lined up perfectly and worked out the way it should have. It's hard to go back now and wish that anything had been different about the way it all went.

ME: Especially because you are between Mike O'Malley, who is amazing, and Nick, who is amazing. If you are looking for reasons to make it easier, you could say that Nick did *The Office*, and blah blah blah.

MIKE: Who knows? Maybe Nick gets a stomach virus while on set and barfs everywhere, and our association with him is unpleasant and we don't want that guy because he barfed everywhere or whatever. Whatever stupid thing could have happened. I saved that Post-it note, and after the show ended, I framed it and gave it to Nick as a parting gift.

I was nothing like Ron Swanson, meanwhile, or at least nothing like the way Nick made him. On the internet you can find a video of how my Ron Swanson sounded, almost wispy as compared to Ron's famous baritone. It wasn't wrong or bad, but it wasn't Ron. That character could've only been played by one guy, and his name is Nick Offerman. "You see someone funny, and you always put them in your back pocket," Greg Daniels told me recently. "I don't think it was the case where it was 'It has to be him and no one else,' but he left such a great impression. He was perfect for it."

Allison Jones, *Casting Director*

Nick Offerman's and Paul Schneider's roles were auditions and metamorphosed with every side's rewrite (and I assume some discussions among writers about how characters were coming together). I believe we had new sides with different character attributes, quite a few iterations of some. It became more about how someone they loved could fit in best. I think Nick's role evolved quite a bit to what they thought was an enigma who collected World War II military weapons.

My Ron audition might not have been perfect, but it was memorable. Sometimes you go into a room and are met by blank expressions, which you intuit as negative. But the chatter was lively in this room. I mentioned my connection to Steve Carell, which made the banter with Greg and Mike less formal. Not just that, but I was making them laugh. The audition involved the scene where Ron spoke about a piece of war memorabilia on his desk, and divine inspiration must've struck in the form of comedic timing, because I was hitting all the beats. *This is good, real good*, I thought as I walked to my car.

I didn't carry the kind of self-doubt that usually overtakes me minutes after leaving an audition. You can imagine the kind: the uncertainty that creeps in and becomes frustration until you're yelling in the car while sitting in traffic about how you screwed it up. How you made all the wrong acting choices while you redo the audition in the rearview mirror, as if that will make it better. Not this time, though: I felt satisfied if not a bit uplifted by my performance, knowing that if I didn't get the role of Ron, which I was sure I wouldn't, then the showrunners might be able to find something for me down the line. Perhaps a juicy guest spot? For a show that seemed like it would have some legs, this was as good a sign as any.

Talking and laughing my way through an audition was a strategy I'd employed, unconsciously, to good effect in the past. Though not always. Some years earlier, I'd been up for a dramatic role in a film. As a journeyman character actor, I understood that my weight and outsized personality led me to be perceived as the "fat funny guy." Actors get labeled all the time, as if someone's rounding out the roster of a high school rom-com—*the friendly neighbor, the realist best friend, the stoner, the cocky athlete.* I'll take any opportunity to show that I'm more than the silly fat dude. As Amy has said to me on more than one occasion, "We're in the most ridiculous profession ever. We perform for other people." Her point? That by showing up to do our work in front of others, we're also continuously setting ourselves up for unfair judgments. But hey, there's nothing else I'd rather do. Or there's nothing else I *can* do.

I was so set on getting this dramatic role and showing another side of my acting skills that I rehearsed ad nauseam, to the distress of those around me. In short, I overprepared.

When it was time to step into that room, I thought I had nailed it . . . but not in the way I'd expected. I engaged in a twenty-minute conversation with the producers and casting director where we talked, laughed, and roasted one another. After the audition, I believed I'd nailed it. Not a doubt in my mind.

An hour after leaving, my agent at the time called me. "How did the audition go?" he asked.

"It went great!" I boasted. "Really, really great. I nailed it. I gotta tell you, I freaking nailed this one."

"Yeah? Well, I have some bad news."

No way.

"You lost the job," Denny said clinically.

"Oh my God, but how?"

"You had *too* much fun. They enjoyed you so much that they couldn't see past the humor and laughter."

It's a lesson I've thought about since: If I go for comedy, I work the room. I make them laugh, I trade stories, I bring up Steve Carell. If I go for a dramatic role? I play it straight. In the years since *Parks* went off the air, I've been called into dramatic auditions and asked by producers to talk about my time on the show, what it was like to improvise with Amy and play patty-cake with Chris Pratt. I respond in the simplest and most straightforward way I know how: "Just a gift." No more emphasis needed. No reason to be denied a role for being funny. "Just a gift for seven straight years," I tell them.

Unfortunately, that gift would not come in the form of playing Ron Swanson, but two weeks later I received a call from Lynda telling me that the producers would like me to audition for the role of Jerry. "You interested?" she asked.

"Lynda, stop asking me stupid questions."

Anyway, when I arrived at the lot, for the Jerry audition this time, the waiting room held the most diverse group of men I'd seen in Hollywood since . . . ever. Generally, when I go to an audition, I'll see guys who look like me. This was different. There were fat guys with short hair, skinny guys with long hair, Indian guys with no hair, Black guys with purple hair. Jerry was a side character at the time, aka a character that is not officially in the script but could be, so the writers, producers, and showrunners didn't know what Jerry would look like. This has a dual effect: On one hand, it means you're not competing against a hundred guys who look like you. On the other, they've widened the proverbial pool, which makes it more difficult to lean into a singular direction.

I was ready this time, though, and less nervous than I'd been before because Mike, Greg, and Allison were already familiar with me. And since as a side character Jerry's lines consisted of random bits that lacked cohesion, I used instinct to guide me. That sensitivity that Jerry carried episode to episode, his nervous posture behind the desk, his shying away from Tom's disapproval? That trait began in that room, perhaps because of my real-life vulnerability.

Allison Jones

We knew that we were going to have folks in the office who were there every week, and I was a huge fan of yours as someone who felt like an enthusiastic, small-town, good-father, smart-worker, hard-worker type (my words, not Mike and Greg's). You fit into what I thought was the universe, and luckily your agent at the time knew we had turned these roles into important roles on The Office. (They took my Phyllis!) Also, you always delivered the comedy in a real way. It was never fake or trying to be funny. You and Retta both. Thrilled to get you both in there.

Two weeks later, I received the call that changed my life.

Lynda again. "Jim, the Untitled Amy Poehler Project would like to book you."

"Oh my gosh . . . for Jerry?"

"For Jerry, yes. Do you want to accept?"

"Lynda, stop asking me stupid questions."

Greg Daniels and Me

GREG: Allison [Jones] would bring people in to read for other roles. I don't know if she knew you were coming in for the role of Ron or if she knew in the back of her head, *Hey, I love this guy; he's a great improviser . . .*

The way I first heard about you is Allison saying, "You gotta know who Jim O'Heir is. He's a Chicago guy and a great improviser, and he's got that background."

ME: I love that.

GREG: To speak about *The Office*, the pitch to Angela [Kinsey], Oscar [Nuñez], and Brian [Baumgartner] was, "Look, you know, you're not necessarily characters in the beginning, but be there, be funny. You're on the set where the home base is and you're going to thrive." So, to hear you say that you were worried you weren't necessarily going to be a character is so silly to me because we always had a plan for you.

ME: I never knew that. A lot of nights' sleep were lost over that.

GREG: I'm so sorry.

Retta, *Donna Meagle*

I got my job *because* I'm a chatter. I had just gotten this new watch and Mike [Schur] commented, "Hey, nice watch," and I quickly fired back, "Oh thank you so much, so there's this website called Gilt Groupe and you have to be invited to be a member and I can totally invite you if you'd like, just give me your email and . . ." I knew right then that Mike thought I was a maniac in the best way and that Greg [Daniels] probably thought I was a maniac in the worst way, but that he loved me anyway.

I did one audition for Donna. So did Octavia Spencer and Yvette Nicole Brown. I didn't hear back for weeks, but I got the call from my manager at the time, who described it as a "glorified extra." At this point, I had done an episode on *Moesha* and a little part on a smaller movie. If somebody had asked me whether I was an actor or a stand-up comedian, I would've said, "I'm a stand-up trying to be an actor."

I was over the moon about working with Amy Poehler. Amy, ten years my junior, is a matriarch of sketch and improvisational comedy, not only through her work on *SNL* but before that in Chicago's Second City and her founding of Upright Citizens Brigade along with Matt Walsh, Matt Besser, and Ian Roberts. Though she's not from Chicago, I often associate Amy with the town in which I grew up and that I love, as well as with the ceaseless talent that has come out of this network—everyone from the previously mentioned Steve Carell to Sean Hayes to freaking Tina Fey. An alumnus of the Second City training program myself, I was ready to learn everything I could from her.

Now, you might be wondering, what got me to that audition room? Allow me to share.

I was born at 1:15 a.m. on February 4, 1962, at St. Francis Hospital in Blue Island, Illinois, to the greatest parents ever, Eileen and John O'Heir. My mother's maiden name was O'Keefe, so the green was running through my body from the very start . . .

Oh God, Jim. Are you kidding me? This is boring. Skip to the good part!

I credit three things with getting me to where I am now. The first is interning for the college radio station at Loyola University in Chicago, WLUW, which encouraged my love for performance and voice work over what I was going to school for, accounting. Yes, accounting. I chose it because I had a few high school buddies who were doing it and it seemed like a secure career choice at the time. Nothing against accountants, but . . . an accountant? I haven't balanced a checkbook in fifty years.

My interest in radio led me to leave Loyola and train with the Midwestern Broadcasting School, which focused on teaching people how to break into the radio industry. Not only how to work on-air but also how to edit, produce, prepare news, and learn just about every job done at a small-town radio station. You graduate with a demo reel as your calling card and a fledgling ambition to pay your dues. Nobody was going to hand me a gig at WLS in Chicago or Z100 in New York when I graduated. Rather, my first entertainment "job" as a DJ was on WRIN-WLQI in Rensselaer, Indiana. It was utter hell. I worked sixty-hour weeks with $120/week take-home pay, *but* I did get to annoy the hell out of local Rensselaerians with my constant rotation of Barry Manilow and Neil Diamond. There was even an hour where I'd feature a "party line," where local farmers would trade animals for equipment, or vice versa, and talk about their daily woes and successes. To make matters worse, I was working for a steaming mess of a boss who always seemed confused and didn't know whether to shit or wind his watch, and I was living in an apartment that was decrepit and roach filled. Still, it was mine and mine alone.

My parents, the most encouraging people who've ever walked the face of the earth, came to visit me during this period. They'd had a conversation on the drive over where they promised each other that they'd support my choices—what I was doing and where I was living. My dad, ever the logical one (though he had a wicked sense of humor, too), explicitly said to my mom, "No matter what, Eileen, we're going to be encouraging. *No matter what.*" When they arrived and looked around the premises, their eyes locked. "It's nice," my mom said plainly. My dad seemed pleased by Mom's demeanor. But then the floodgates of motherhood opened. "Oh my God, Jimmy," she cried, "I don't know what we ever did to make you want to live like this. What did we do, will you tell me?"

Within two weeks of that visit, my mom and aunt snuck into town and found me a better place to live. That's the kind of support I've always been blessed with.

Perhaps not as supportive was the young cashier at the supermarket when I went to cash a check one day. When she saw my name on the check, she asked, "Youuuuuu're Jim O'Heir?"

"Yes, ma'am!" My first time ever being "seen" in public. I was "feeling myself," as the kids say.

"Oh." Her face sank. "I didn't think you'd look like that."

And . . . back to reality.

Between my mom blaming herself for my living situation and this cashier shaming my good looks, I was beginning to think that Rensselaer, Indiana, was not the place for me.

I received a call one day at the station. A man said he traveled back and forth to see his kid at St. Joseph's College and always enjoyed listening to my program while on the road. He suggested that if I was ever looking to do something different, I should consider training with Second City in Chicago. This was the pre-cell-phone era, so it was touching that this guy had pulled over to make a phone call from a diner to some local station host. It was the type of call that, in retrospect, you imagine was fated to happen. Because it could've gone the other way, too—a stranger could've called up the station and pronounced me an unfunny piece of crap.

After I had done my time and paid my dues at the radio station, I decided to take the stranger's advice and apply to Second City, where comedy was the goal. Those laughs were as good as money. The exact moment I knew I wanted to do this acting "thing" for the rest of my life arrived on the main stage during a class led by Martin de Maat, an improv guru who died way too young. Here I was performing on the same stage as legends like John Belushi, Bill Murray, Mary Gross, Mike Myers, and Gilda Radner, to name a few, when it happened: I got my first laugh. It was in a room full of newbies like me, so the bar for impressing them was admittedly low, but I'd done an original bit that my peers loved. I often return to that moment because, like the friendly call to the radio station, the positive response made me consider the alternative. What if it hadn't gone my way? What if I'd bombed class after class? At that moment, I never thought that acting would pay the bills, but I knew that somehow, some way, I would always need to perform in front of an audience.

One day, I took a class led by Arlene Golonka, famous for playing Millie on *The Andy Griffith Show*, who said to me after a particularly dramatic scene, "Jim, you don't belong here." I was mortified, wrongly thinking she was disappointed by my performance. She clarified, "You need to go much higher than this class. You need to aspire to this. To drama." Arlene's statement made me consider how I'd been hiding behind comedy for so long, using it as a mask to cover my weight issues, which stemmed from an early age. She said the transition from comedy to drama could provide a professional challenge, one she thought I was ready for. Although I loved comedy, and always would, Arlene reminded me that it didn't need to be my single pathway in entertainment.

So, there was the radio station in Rensselaer, Indiana; my "moment" onstage at Second City; and then . . . then there was *Stumpy's Gang*. For those of you who don't know what *Stumpy's Gang* is, which I'm guessing is all but ten people reading this book, permit me to tell you the plot by borrowing from *Variety*'s November 1, 1994, review, published after we had moved the stage show to Los Angeles, three years after debuting it in Chicago:

```
Play is set at GenetiCo, a fictional bio-
engineering firm where the evil Dr. Minkley
(Ned Crowley) is hard at work churning
out mutant "specimens," most of which are
destined for the incinerator. At the literal
bottom of the GenetiCo hierarchy is bio-
maintenance disposal engineer (read janitor)
Frank Bubman (Jim O'Heir), who rescues a
few of the hapless specimens—not out of any
sense of human kindness, but strictly for
his own entertainment. Frank's particular
form of entertainment is a fantasy TV puppet
show, "Stumpy's Gang," a twisted melange of
children's shows from the '50s. Tormented by
the memory of his cruel German mother (Desmond
Rouge), Frank sets out to restage Wagner's Ring
cycle with the help of his mutant specimens,
```

whom he has named Stumpy, Gristle, and Booger.
When co-workers Chuck (Michael LoPrete) and
Nora (Mary-Kathleen Gordon) discover the
"gang," we're off to the races.

I'll stop there. I also have to look up the word "mélange."
Damn writers . . .

Me, as Frank Bubman in the shocking play Stumpy's Gang, which became a cult classic. Just to be clear, the mutant is on the left.

Stumpy's Gang was the most delightful mess I've ever been a part of. It's part gross-out, part apocalyptic reverie, part manic dream cycle, part horror-fantasy, part comedic puppet show, and part parts, literally, with dicks and bloody corpses and limbs and expanding labia. I loved every minute of it. For one thing, it was more radical than anything I'd ever done. As odd as the *Chicago Reader** or *Variety* found it then, it has since become a cult classic in the way *The Room* or *Troll 2* has, except for one key fact: way fewer people have seen it.

---

* "The grotesquely ursine Jim O'Heir adds a new dimension to the role of the enfant terrible with his uninhibited and enthusiastic portrayal of Frank, who will break your heart even as he turns your stomach."

The show hit an inflection point, however, when one day, as I drove down Clark Street to Stage Left Theatre, I spotted a huge line, with a couple people even dressed as my character from the show, Frank. These must've been people who'd seen the show at least once before, and they weren't the types to be turned off by incinerators and blood; they reveled in it. However, when we moved the show to Los Angeles a couple years later, we had to warn viewers in the front row that they *might* get splashed with fake blood (read: they *would* get splashed). LA theatergoers don't like getting splashed with anything if they're not warned prior.

Stumpy's Gang taught me that the road to stardom is often long, surprising, and splattered with blood. But it was also my ticket to Los Angeles, where—*flash forward*—twenty-odd years later, and through years of countless guest spots and failed auditions to being fortunate enough to work with mega talents like Leslie Nielsen, Holly Hunter, and Swoosie Kurtz, I received the call that changed the trajectory of my acting career, and my life. I'd officially been booked on the Untitled Amy Poehler Project, or whatever name it had morphed into.

Was I excited? *Yes.*

Inspired? *Of course.*

Grateful? *Definitely.*

Still terrified? *Absolutely.*

Another Member of the Fam

Although I'd worked on the CBS Studio Center lot many times—known in the biz as CBS Radford—this was my first time returning to the premises since the network had done a major overhaul of their buildings. The place looked brand-spanking-new, which added to my cautious excitement for my first table read on the Untitled Amy Poehler Project.

After five or so minutes into waiting, the elevators opened to reveal six people: Amy, Rashida, Nick, Aubrey Plaza, Paul, and some Hollywood newcomer named Aziz. They were, I assumed, my new cast members. I only recognized Amy and Rashida, and Rashida only because I was a fan of *The Office*. I'd never laid eyes on the others in my life.

Their laughter and lively conversation filled the hallways as they walked toward me. I later learned that they'd just come from an HR seminar about workplace harassment in which sketches from *SNL* were used as examples of what not to do. I'm not sure how much they learned.

I fastened on a smile and righted my posture, as if they were about to come in for a group hug, but they only offered nods and half smiles. They obviously had no idea who I was, and why should they? I was a random guy in a waiting room, and they were chummy new friends on the way to creating something brilliant.

I felt deflated. I didn't think I stood a chance of being part of their club. I texted a friend, **Maybe this isn't going to be what I thought it would.** Over the past two weeks, he had listened to me talk endlessly about this new role and being able to work with one of my idols, Amy Poehler. Since she and the others barely acknowledged me, I believed that this would be a short-term gig. I texted on: **Maybe this is just a job. Maybe it lasts a couple episodes, nothing more. Maybe I go in and do my job and go home . . .**

My friend responded with a smiley face and some affirmative balm for the soul: **Dude, relax.**

Turned out he was right. I was getting too much in my head, because a few minutes later, Mike Schur returned to the waiting room with a winning grin. "Come on in, Jim," he said, and he led me to what I would find out later was the writers' hangout area.

The cast sat on couches arranged in a semicircle, chatting up a storm. Mike interrupted with a "Hey, hey, hey!" The group turned to face Mike, me beside him. "I want to introduce you to another member of the family. Everyone, this is Jim O'Heir."

I expected crickets. Or the opposite of crickets: no noise whatsoever. But within seconds, all of them welcomed me with a smattering of "hello"s, "hey"s, "howdy"s, and "How the heck are ya, Jim?"s. Maybe I'd become a member of the club after all.

In the beginning, table reads were hosted in the basement of the CBS Radford soundstage, but as the show continued, we moved to the third floor, where the writers had their offices. I'm not sure why we originally met in the basement, but the idea that we could only go up is as apt a metaphor as any.

The basement was not like the kind I remember as a kid growing up in Chicago, full of those weird jumping bugs and home videos wrapped in cobwebs. Like the rest of the newly renovated lot, it was orderly and clean. The actors, writers, producers, network executives, and even production staff (hair, makeup, props, camera) sat around the room, and the sheer volume of people created a line of energy that you could follow around the perimeter, like one of those lasers in *Ghostbusters*.

Since Greg Daniels was still showrunning *The Office*, it was Mike Schur's job to lead the table read, which he did with a curt introduction before narrating everything in the script except the dialogue, where actors stepped in. Amy cracked up the room on nearly every page. Where some of us were nervous to read our lines—having not had the time to develop our characters' traits—I like to think that Leslie's brash confidence was starting to be developed as early as this read, and Amy had the lines, opportunities, and talent to strike comedic gold.

The jokes never get as big a laugh as they do during the table read. All the writers are there and intent on hooting and hollering for the jokes their colleagues wrote. Then there are the network executives who want to believe everything they're pouring money into is funny, which was easy considering this first script for the aptly named "Pilot" *was* funny. I mean really funny. The episode is Leslie-centric, to the point that it feels as if Amy is doing stand-up for most of it. Not once did it disappoint. When working with such a talented lead actor like Amy, it can be incredibly intimidating, but I think we all nailed it.

Greg Daniels

I think we got a lot right with the pilot, but it wasn't matched to Amy's energy perfectly. The vibe in politics at that time was very optimistic because Obama had been elected, and Amy's character had a lot of Hillary energy to her [*laughs*], and there are a lot of pluses and minuses to Hillary, but we were maybe leaning into a little naivete and foolishness and over-optimism and maybe not getting what people were doing around her.

Almost always, on TV, a show starts off with greater

conflicts among its characters than at the end because by the end the characters start to know each other better and viewers fall in love with them. Shows generally go in the direction of greater love between its people. But our early notes on Aziz referred to him as "the schemer," this Machiavellian guy who was abusing politics to get his own ends, a little lieutenant who's kind of undermining her. And Ron, the concept behind him was that he was a libertarian who didn't believe in government but that he was Leslie's boss—that she had all this enthusiasm, but he didn't believe in the process to begin with. We were worried that this wasn't realistic, so we talked with some city planners to gain perspective. We talked to a city planner in Pasadena who was a libertarian [laughs]. Turns out our joke of an idea turned out to be real.

Greg Levine

There was a time where Greg [Daniels] and Mike [Schur] were thinking that the show would take place in public service of some kind, though they didn't know exactly what that meant. They were obsessed with The Wire, for good reason, and they thought about how to make a comedy version of The Wire. How do you do a show that's less a situational comedy and more about a "project" that unites everyone? In The Wire, you're seeing how all these different elements of Baltimore come together. The idea for Parks' [season 1] then was: How do you fill in this empty lot? How do you fill in the pit? At one point, there was serious consideration that the show would be called Lot 48 because there it was thought that this lot would unite everyone. They wanted to do a show set in a place that could represent anywhere in the world, and they picked a place on the map, and it was in Indiana.

I did the research for these guys. I called parks departments in various areas that were like the town they were thinking and asked them this: "How do you build a park?" They would give me every detail and I would ask, "Well, which agencies did you talk to?" I'd call these agencies, which is where I learned how important city planners are to the development of a park. My research fed into the types of characters that Greg and Mike were thinking about creating. At the time, I had a friend who was an aide to a city mayor, so Mike, Greg, and I took a field trip to LA city hall and sat in on a public forum. That was the first time they realized that a public forum could also be a comedy space.

In a few months' time, I had become an expert on all things bureaucratic, and I organized these notes into topics and characters based on Greg and Mike's vision and created a binder full of this idea-vomit that I would give to writers that came on board.

Greg Daniels

The theme of the show is going to be a project, we thought; it was going to be filling in the pit. Maybe the show should be called *The Pit*, we thought at one point. Part of that was to keep it separate from *The Office*—so you're connecting Leslie with actual constituents and not just all these people working in the Parks Department. Which is how we get Rashida. It's how we get Chris Pratt.

Morgan Sackett, *Producer*

"Okay, so now we have to come up with a pit we're going to have for seven years." They told me that I was unflappable about it, that it didn't seem to faze me, but I remember leaving a lunch when we'd discussed this and thinking, *Well, someone's gonna talk them out of that idea. That'll never happen. I'm not that worried about it.*

I found the pit. I found a lot of pits. I convinced Greg to go with the one we did because some of the others were out in Sierra Madre. This was during the financial crisis, and on the first day of digging the pit, the lot was foreclosed on. We just took it over, ended up paying the bank directly instead of the person we were renting from.

I had heard stories about Greg and Mike's nonstop work ethic, of how they spent their free time figuring out how to make a show hit even harder, but seeing them up close was like watching a magic act. You could see the preparation that went into it but still not understand how it was done. They made the hard work feel flawless by nature of their good humor and charm. (They also provided lots of snacks.) The commitment to their actors never wavered, whether we were at a table read, in-scene shooting, or in conversations about our characters after the fact. Greg said he approached character-building from a playwriting perspective. He would routinely ask himself and his fellow writers, "What's our topic? What are our themes? How do you get different personifications of attitudes about these themes?" He told me how he compared the characters he was developing to those on *The West Wing* but imagined them with much lower stakes—somebody like Leslie Knope believing that what she's doing is super-important,

Sister Beth and her fam visiting the set. They only came for the craft services.

Mike Schur sporting a Red Sox pullover, as obsessive a writer and showrunner as he is a sports fan.

high-stakes government work, but at the end of the day she's in the Parks Department in a small town in Indiana. Stuff like that.

Greg and Mike kept open avenues of conversation and answered any questions we had about our characters. Even though they were firm believers in the amazing scripts that the writers created (themselves included), they were often loose with respect to how we actors approached character decisions, and they frequently encouraged improv.

My first improv moment came on the first day of shooting when Amy went around to the Parks Department's employees to, per Greg's instructions, "shoot the shit with us." You know, stuff like, "Talk to Ron about what's atop his desk," or "Talk to Tom about weird Tom stuff." Although this exercise wasn't in the script, Greg thought it would serve as a fruitful character-building session. If something rich came of it that could be captured on film, then even better.

The cameras started rolling. When it came time for Leslie to stop by my desk, I kept repeating a mantra in my head: *Please be funny, please be funny, please, for the love of God, be funny.* You might think my prior experience at Second City would've provided an advantage if not a type of self-assurance, but Second City, though big, was still a regional opportunity. This was network television, the big leagues.

Leslie began by asking Jerry about the stuff on his desk, and it felt like the separation between me and my character melted away as soon as she posed the question. In other words, I was feeling less self-conscious.

I looked to my left and then my right and spotted an empty glass jar on the desk, thinking that that object could inspire some line of thought. "It's my swear jar," I told Leslie, indicating a jar devoid of cash or change. I thought it was clever. Amy did, too, because she chuckled.

Minutes after Leslie finished going around the room and greeting other characters, Greg approached me and offered a pithy piece of criticism: "We'll need to find your rhythm, Jim." He didn't say anything beyond that, leaving his seven words to ring inside my brain.

And the faith I'd had in my swear jar statement (a funny line, I've been told) evaporated, and I spent the remaining hours playing over in my head what I could've said—no, what I *should've* said.

Meanwhile, what was Greg thinking?

Greg Daniels

I'll say this: as a director, I was probably too much of a writer while I was directing because, well, that doesn't sound like the best thing to tell an actor [*laughs*]. But I was thinking like a writer, I was thinking, *Okay, so this guy is here. Now, what's his role in the play?*, you know what I mean? What's his point of view? How's he going to be funny? I knew you could do it. It was just trying to find the character, since characters change so much. It's like *King of the Hill*, which I know you like. Dale Gribble? That character didn't gel for me until the third episode, where the boys go hunting and shoot a rare bird and Dale just rats his friends out and runs. I was like, "There we are! That's who he is!" So, in the first season, I was always thinking about how characters would reveal themselves. I was thinking about their comic engines. Still, you're not supposed to share that internal thinking with the cast! [*Laughs*]

Cocreator Greg Daniels with his "director's cap" on. He's brilliant, smart, kind, caring . . . okay, you get the idea.

Okay, so now you and I both know what Greg meant by "find your rhythm." The ultimate writer-director-showrunner was helping me fully flesh out Jerry as a character, for which I'm grateful.

To this day, I don't enjoy wardrobe fittings. I convince myself the designer is judging me the second I walk in for being a bigger dude, even if, in reality, there's no judgment coming from anybody except myself. It's the fear that, for the next hour or two, I'm going to be exposed and vulnerable in front of a stranger. You know that feeling of dancing for the first time at a middle school end-of-year party, where the lights are barely turned low and you don't know what the hell you're doing and you're sure that everyone is watching? When slow dancing meant putting your heads on each other's shoulders? I feel that same awkwardness in wardrobe fittings, the difference being that the lights are turned on very bright. I've done hundreds of wardrobe fittings over the years, and each one gives me anxiety.

One of the early fittings during *Parks'* first season was no different except for one crucial element: the costume designer Kirston Leigh Mann had brought out several outfits and talked about costumes Jerry *might* wear on future episodes.

WHAT? Future episodes?

For a guest role, which this still was at the time, it's not uncommon to try on a few outfits and call it a day. The designer sends the pics over to the producers, who choose what you'll be wearing for that week's episode. Trying on a few outfits would've been more than adequate and was what I'd been expecting. But Kirston brought out multiple outfits that Jerry would wear "*should* he return for more episodes," she told me at the time. Maybe Kirston knew something I didn't, but either way it filled me with hope.

I looked ridiculous in each one. You see, stars like Amy and Rashida have earned the confidence to refuse an outfit if it's not to their liking. They say no by virtue of being the stars of the show. In my case, the desire to get out of there as quickly as possible often motivates me to say yes. Once, I arrived at my dressing room to find a pair of khakis and a red polo waiting for me. I changed into them but noticed that the shirt was small. I mean comically small. A rational person would've taken it off and brought it to the attention of the wardrobe department. But not me. I wasn't going to be a troublemaker, and if they thought that's what I should wear, then damn it, that's what I was going to wear. And so I did. Later, I ran into Kirston, and she asked me how everything felt.

I sucked in my stomach and said, "A little tight, not gonna lie."

"I'm not surprised," she said. "That's Nick's outfit." There was a wardrobe mix-up and his outfit landed in my dressing room. By the time I pointed out the ill fit to Kirston, I'd already shot a scene in the clothing. (You can peep this malfunction in the episode "The Camel.")

We had a big laugh about that one.

As we kept shooting episodes over the first season, I gradually found my groove, owing much of that to Greg, Mike, Amy, and Retta. Retta became my loyal sounding board during these early days and for the rest of our time on *Parks*. She and I shared the circumstances of having guest roles with no clear future in sight. As a result, we'd return to our respective dressing rooms after shooting and share stories like kids returning from an epic day of summer camp, full of winsome, wide-eyed enthusiasm.

"Oh my God," Retta would say during these early shoots, "I was so nervous today. I almost died."

"You have no idea," I'd reply. "I was shaking. Literally shaking."

Retta is a comedian and had little improv experience. Before she and I were made full-time cast members, she was still traveling between shoots to perform stand-up at clubs around the country. To this day, I don't understand how she kept up that pace during those early years.

I had tried stand-up a few times in my twenties, while in Indiana and working at the radio station. One time, at an open-mic night, I overheard one of the "featured comics" tell the MC, "I can't go on after that guy," pointing at me. "He's gonna do all the fat jokes. I need to go on first." I decided right then that the stand-up world, particularly the open-mic one from which so many comics emerge, was not for me. Not that acting is any more promising: for every ten auditions you do, you may get only one callback. Rejection, rejection, rejection.

This is all to say that I greatly respected Retta—her poise, her ability to show up despite uncertainty, her good humor, her friendship. And let me tell you, she and I had a lot of time to chat. Since we were filming in a new part of the Radford lot, she and I were placed in these fancy new dressing rooms while the mainstays worked

Just me and my girl Retta.

from your typical trailers. These dressing rooms were beautiful. They were spacious, clean, modern, and inviting. So beautiful that Retta and I actually felt bad for the stars, what with their having to fit into those suffocating bathrooms with bad plumbing and all. Retta reminded me recently that by the time we had become series regulars, around season 3, at which point the producers wanted to give us the same trailers as the rest of the gang, she wanted to tell them not to bother. Our dressing rooms were nicer than the trailers.

Retta emerged as a real buddy and confidant in these dressing rooms. Equally scared and equally paid, we bonded over stories of our past—shows we'd worked on, parts we'd gotten or wished we had, parts we wished we hadn't, and times in which we were ready to hang it up forever. She became my work wife and I her work husband, and as work husband I took pride in getting to fetch us treats from the food trucks.

I credit Retta with comforting me during periods of uncertainty. Take this one: After we finished the first season, there was a wrap party at some hot new club off Hollywood Boulevard, where Retta and I were not among the cast invited onstage to cut the cake. This shouldn't have surprised me—but it didn't hurt any less, especially since the cast had done so much to make me feel welcome, including coming to visit me and Retta at our fancy dressing rooms.

Chief among these visitors was Paul Schneider (who played Mark Brendanawicz), who had become a key advocate for our inclusion on the show. In between takes, while Retta and I passed the time, Paul would come by, make himself cozy on the couch, and share his own impressions of how things were shaping up. "You guys are killing it out there," he'd say. "You need to do *more*."

We leaned in, nervously sipping our coffee.

"What I mean," he'd say, "is they have to learn how to use you guys more. You're fucking hilarious, and I think you're being underutilized."

If Paul had been lying and saying these things just to be nice, it still would've been enough. His appraisal humbled us and indicated we were being noticed by another actor, a lead one no less. It had a profound effect on our confidence.

In retrospect, perhaps *not* being a series regular like Paul made me feel less pressure. By the end of season 1 I had begun to feel more content to just seep into the background like the Stanleys and Phyllises and Oscars of *The Office* fame. That show was still going strong, and our ratings were being compared to theirs week to week. *Be an Oscar*, I told myself. *Be present. Be content.*

Being there and on set, it turned out, was easy to do, especially when I could get onto the Wi-Fi during scenes in the office. I found plenty of time to browse the computer and make my character "look busy." So did Retta. She would shop—God knows how many purses she bought during that first season—while I'd play online games. When that became tedious, I tried to make the crew laugh—there was always time to have some fun amid the hard work. During one shoot, I pretended to pick my ear with my little finger and then take a whiff, which they kept in the final episode. (You can see this take place behind Tom in "Smallest Park.")

I remember so much dicking around during this time that the term "dicking around" took on a literal context. In between takes, we would doodle at our desks. What is it about doodling that makes one feel compelled to draw a dick? That's a serious question. The number of dicks drawn—by me, by Pratt, and even by Aubrey—would put Jonah Hill's character in *Superbad* to shame. Dicks on every piece of paper you could find. It's a miracle none ended up in any of the episodes. Even one of our camera guys, Will Emery, who also happened to be a fantastic artist, drew dicks. Oh boy, could Will draw a dick.

All dicking around aside, there was a feeling of "figuring it out as we went along" that went into the first season. Greg and Mike would have conversations on set with us about character development. It seemed most of us "needed to find our rhythm," especially when our six-episode order was renewed for a full-length second season. That was the great news. The not-so-great news was viewer feedback about Leslie's character and how she appeared too much like Michael from *The Office*, a fear Greg had had since the show's conception. In one dismissive review, *Collider* wrote, "*Parks and Recreation* is a swell little show that is still figuring out exactly what it wants to be. Fans of *The Office* will likely enjoy the program but most will likely consider it as a weak little sister." *Fine.* For Leslie Knope to be less a little sister and *Parks* to be more itself than *The Office*, it needed to focus on friendships, which is where I believe the show finds steady, soulful, and funny footing. Luckily, we were all getting closer on and off set.

Mike Schur

We were in a position of extreme privilege when it came to the process by which shows were made. Then, almost instantly, it flipped, and we were kicked in the face, down and out, and being knifed by critics. Everyone felt that this show wasn't *The Office*, and that it's not funny, and Amy's not Steve, and this idea isn't good, and whatever. Amy calls that, even to this day, being at the bottom of Show Mountain. She's like, "We are at the bottom of Show Mountain, and we have to very steadily scratch and claw and climb our way up, and prove to people that we deserve to live." Every year, we got to the end of the season, and we didn't know whether we were coming back. We never took any of it for granted because we almost got canceled so many times that every day we got to do another episode, we were like, "Oh my God, we get to do this again. This is incredible."

This is one example of this. I don't know if you remember, but at the end of the second season, Amy got pregnant again. We realized that based on her due date, we were not going to be able to start shooting new episodes when we normally would have, in late July or early August to have them ready to go on in September. We went to NBC and said, "If you want us to come back next year, what you need to do is pick up the show now, in January, and we'll finish the twenty-four-episode season we were going to do and keep going. We will shoot six more, and we will bank them and have them ready to air in September and October. And then, by the time those run out, Amy will be able to come back, and we'll be able to shoot more and keep going." They said yes. They picked the show up early and we finished that twenty-four-episode season and went right into season 3. So we basically made thirty episodes that second season, which is bananas.

Then, while we were making those six episodes, they decided to move the show to midseason and not have it debut in September after all, which meant we didn't have to do what we did. At the time, moving to midseason meant you were dead. They were basically saying we are going to cancel the show. We are not going to give you any of the fanfare that comes with launching in September, and you're not going to get a splashy debut with all the advertising and everything else. I remember talking to the writers and telling them what was going on and basically said, "Look, we don't know what this means; it's possible that this is good somehow. It's possible that the show they want to put on instead of us bombs, and then by the time we come back, people are like, 'Thank God, that show that I like is back.'" All we could do is put our heads down, do our jobs, and make the episodes as good as they can possibly be, air them, and hope for the best. That is exactly what we did. We made the best episodes we could. What that means is that we were not holding anything back. Any idea that we had ever had for the distant future—for season 5, say—all of that went out the window. We were doing it right now because we needed to leave it all on the court. We had no reason to delay. Andy and April had kind of gotten together at the end of season 2, and we were like, "Screw it, they're getting married. Because that's more exciting and more fun." Can we do it? We did it.

That's the way we kind of wrote the show for the rest of the time it was on. What that did, I think, when you watch it now, is we never run in place. We were never killing time. There is always something very big and juicy happening in Leslie Knope's life, whether it's personal or professional, or both, and that gives the show this real sense of forward motion that makes it exciting.

Bond . . .
Parks
Bond

Season 2's "The Camel" shows the Parks Department banding together to commission a mural, at the same time convincing the audience of Leslie's selflessness and compassion. "Galentine's Day" not only solidified the gals' friendship, but it launched a national holiday at the same time. (February 13, mark your calendars!) And "The Possum" helped establish Andy's new feelings for April and their adorkable goofiness. Could I see that the scripts were stronger than the first season and that the writers had begun to realize the secret ingredient to making *Parks* different from *The Office* was to make it sweeter? I could, and I also noticed that the friendships we were forming away from the soundstage were translating on-screen.

Take my first dinner outing with none other than Chris Pratt. The evening before we filmed season 2's episode 15, "Sweetums," Pratt and I went out following that day's table read. We dined at Laurel Tavern, a favorite of mine, where he ordered the bone marrow, and I the cheeseburger with their excellent crispy fries. Bone marrow makes sense for a stud like Pratt. Cheeseburger for the regular guy, please!

Pratt and I would share many meals over the years, but it was this first outing where we shared our thoughts on the inaugural season and traded tales of how we ended up on this strangely wonderful journey together. In our second season, and with a larger slate of episodes to shoot—not to mention higher expectations for those episodes to perform well, as we were still battling the critical response—we were developing a real friendship. Despite Pratt's rising stardom, he never let go of that boyish charm that many, like me, have been graced by. But on this night at Laurel Tavern, as he devoured that bone marrow, licking it dry, he was no longer a boy wonder. He was an eating machine.

Pratt and I absconded with a golf cart and fled the set . . .
They caught up with us.

While chowing down, Pratt received a call. He checked to see who was calling, at first annoyed. When he registered the number, he perked up. "It's my agent calling," he said. "She never calls. I've got to take this." Chris was in a spot not dissimilar to mine at the time, and even though subsequent years have brought him celebrity and accolades (and rock-hard abs), he's still the modest person I dined with at Laurel Tavern.

Chris Pratt, *Andy Dwyer*

I had done this TV show *Everwood*, which was a four-year run, and I was eager to break into film. I had done one movie called *Take Me Home Tonight*—it was the one I met Anna [Faris] on actually. I was playing the fifth lead in that movie, wasn't on the poster or anything, but I had done a good turn on it, which had gotten me new representation. And by the time I got new representation, an audition came up to play this character—it was a guest star, not a series regular.

The deal was six episodes, in and out, some work for a few weeks; at that point, I was in a bit of a dry spell. I'd gotten close on things, but I was in a place where I couldn't really book anything. This came along and I was happy to take a special-guest-star credit, so I auditioned.

It was wild. I think it was one of those scenarios where it was written for somebody else, but I gave a great audition and got the job. Halfway through shooting the first season, some testing came out that said we were being compared too closely to *The Office*. So, the writers did this break and figured out what wasn't working and what was, and at the end of it I was told they wanted to keep me on as a regular.

It goes back to Allison Jones. I owe her big-time. She was always bringing me in for stuff, putting me in front of the movers and shakers of the comedy world, and she had her finger on the pulse of those comedy auditions. I got so close with her—I don't think I ever got cast in anything—but I got close with her so many times that she was just like, "It's only a matter of time." I was grateful. Turns out they liked me, and I got to be a regular.

Not long ago, a mutual acquaintance was working on a new film with Chris when she called me to tell me how "nice, like really nice," he is. To which I said, "Okay, yeah, we get it. He's talented, hot, and nice. He's got it all. WE GET IT!" Chris is as kindhearted as you can be. He recently texted me out of the blue to tell me I was in a dream he had.

"Did I die in it?" I asked him.

"Actually, you did," he said. "That's why I called you. I wanted to make sure you're okay."

That's a good friend.

I went home after dinner that evening, buoyed by our lively conversation and excited for tomorrow's shoot for an episode called "Sweetums." Among other things, we'd be moving Aziz's Tom out of his house and into a new one (which happens to be the office, temporarily). But when I woke up the next morning to go to work, I was seized by a stomach pain that had nowhere else to go except out (of two holes at once).

I texted Pratt right away: **Dude, are you feeling okay? I feel awful!**

Pratt wrote back: **Feel fine dude. What's wrong?**

It's my stomach. I think I'm dying. Shitting and throwing up at the same time.

Worst of all, I had to be on set in forty minutes. Forget about being on set; I didn't even think I could make it to the car.

I made it to the studio by the grace of God and slightly less traffic than normal, and it only took Susie Flower, the first AD (assistant director), a few seconds of looking at my pale face for her to know that something was terribly wrong. With true organizational proficiency, she did everything to try to make me feel better—bringing me water and tea; making sure I had a private bathroom in the house we were shooting in so I didn't have to lumber (or run) back to my trailer; and taking time out of her busy schedule to make sure I was cared for.

You might ask, rightly so, why I showed up in the first place. *Don't actors get sick days?* Sure they do, but if you're Jim O'Heir and on a week-to-week contract, you show up. Not showing up would inconvenience that day's schedule and personnel, meaning that scripts might have to be rewritten and shots reblocked. Naturally, producers might decide to leave me out of an episode entirely, and that wasn't a fate I wanted to test when I was on the so-called cutting board, as I thought at the time. In all our seasons, Amy didn't miss a shoot. Not once. I wasn't going to be *that guy* simply because I was awfully sick.

For much of the shoot, I was grateful to Susie for her bathroom placement because . . . I was using it liberally. Remember that *Curb Your Enthusiasm* episode where a receptionist obsessively monitors the frequency of Larry's bathroom use? My situation felt like Larry's, and I kept trying to sneak to and from the bathroom when I wasn't needed on set to avoid the curious glances of the cast.

I thought I had finally gotten a handle on the situation by the end of the day. We were filming one of the last scenes, the one where we're moving Tom's stuff from his house to the truck, and I felt slightly better. Not better-better but slightly. Some color had returned to my face, and I had begun to joke a bit more with the cast, who were as concerned about my health as Susie was. Marrow-eating Pratt kept apologizing to me, as if the whole ordeal was somehow his fault. I told him no way. Shooting this last scene was like seeing the finish line a few yards ahead: it meant that I could complete the race and drive home and pass out and cocoon in the privacy of my bed.

And here, my friends, is where my story's dulcet, somewhat hopeful tone turns sour. While "moving" Tom's boxes into the truck, which involved bending, squatting, raising, and cradling, my stomach decided it would relapse. As the episode's director, Dean Holland, called action, I squatted down to pick up a box, and something happened in my pants. I'll spare you the details, but I couldn't just call a time-out and announce to my peers, "Sorry, guys, but can we have a do-over? I pooped myself," so I continued what I had begun, despite the discomfort.

When shooting wrapped, I tidied myself up in the only way I knew how, by fleeing the scene, jumping in my car, and speeding west until I reached home. The lesson? Sometimes you shit the bed and sometimes you shit your pants, but the show must go on.

Chris Pratt

No freaking way, Jim . . . I vaguely remember this . . .
Wow. Just wow.

While we were growing close as a cast, changes were afoot. Given that Greg Daniels was still the showrunner of both *Parks* and *The Office*, and that *The Office* was gearing up for a huge reveal or anticlimax depending on who you ask (Steve

Carell's decision to leave the show), Greg decided he couldn't be in two places at once and would focus solely on his *Office* responsibilities.

His absence during our second season was slightly disappointing at first. When you lose a creative ringleader like Greg, it can feel like you're running around blindfolded and aimless. As intimidatingly smart as Greg was, his sensitivity and compassion drove us to figure things out together. He didn't yell. He didn't demand. But his ambition for high-quality content made us all aspire to meet his expectations.

Greg's departure, though, allowed other members to shine. For one thing, Mike stepped up in a huge way, as did producer Morgan Sackett, whom Greg Daniels called the greatest line producer he's ever worked with. For those of you who don't know, a line producer is the money person who works the budget and deals with almost all aspects of production. They're involved in location scouting, hiring of the department heads, approving the crews, and generally making sure that everything runs smoothly. It was Morgan who found the pit and was responsible for maintaining it—not a little or inexpensive task!

Morgan Sackett

I started as a PA and then I got a job on *Seinfeld* and then I started producing. I did one drama in my life, and it was a disaster. It came out right around the time of *Grey's Anatomy*— it was about the Supreme Court—and at the last minute they did this big rewrite of it where suddenly there's a swimming pool in the Supreme Court for some reason and they're all having sex and it made no sense. It was too bad because it was a good idea. I thought I needed a break from network TV, so I got a job at Disney producing a documentary about sailing—I grew up sailing on a lake in Iowa. I'm no Captain Ahab or anything. We had twelve million dollars to make a documentary about sailing, which even today is a ridiculous number. Dave Rogers, who directed one episode of *Parks*, was a good friend of mine, was now cutting *The Office*. Dave recommended me.

During late 2009 into 2010, Morgan showed up on set with the self-assurance and authority that comes with age and experience. Except that Morgan was only in his midthirties, with the chiseled chin and side-swept hair of a star attorney. Whenever he walked on set, the cast would hush one another and say, "Quiet! Dad's here." Or "Shhh, shhh, the principal is coming." Sometimes he found this funny. Other times, we got the Morgan stare. You did *not* want the Morgan stare. A line producer's job (among many) was to keep an eye on the money. If he was looking at his watch, that meant it was time to get serious.

Morgan is one of my favorite people. I never thought of him as a typical line producer. He was involved in every aspect of production, so it's no surprise that eventually he became an executive producer. He deserves a lot of credit for the show's success. With Greg gone and Mike running point, Morgan stepped in with capable hands to make sure we were all getting the work done. It was Morgan, after all, who told me the best news I'd heard in years—that I would be getting my very own A-story, or main storyline, during the second season. In episode 19, "Park Safety," Jerry claims to be mugged during what was supposed to be a pleasant stroll through the park. I say "claims"

From left to right: Mike Schur, Aubrey Plaza, Morgan Sackett, and a Li'l Sebastian impersonator.

because Jerry makes up the mugging to cover up his embarrassment about falling into a creek. This is also the episode featuring Andy Samberg, who plays the loudmouthed park security ranger who's oblivious of his voice's volume. (I think of the Austin Powers line "I'm having difficulty controlling THE VOLUME OF MY VOICE!")

Jerry's A-story spurs two other plotlines: Leslie coming to the sad realization that her park has a safety issue and soliciting the help of Carl to address it, and Ron teaching a self-defense course to the rest of the department so that they don't end up victims like Jerry. Jerry's concocting the story of the mugging is indicative of his insecurity when it comes to relating to his colleagues. In one exchange in the hospital, when Ron asks Jerry what happened, Jerry says pitifully, "You guys are just gonna laugh." Tom can't help himself: "Why?" he asks. "Did you throw out your shoulder trying to swing a honey pot off your hand?" Leslie takes the bait and laughs. Ron goes on to ask Jerry, "Did you hit him in the beanbag? There's no shame in hitting a criminal in the beanbag."

It's hard not to laugh at Jerry. In one of my favorite scenes of the entire series, when the office is trying so hard not to laugh at him, per Leslie's instruction, Jerry commits a string of faux pas—tripping over a chair, saying "twout" instead of "trout," and bending over, ripping his pants, and farting. Then there's the photo he accidentally shows after finally managing to get his computer plugged in, a solo shot of his "vacation in Muncie." *Classic Jerry.*

Jerry might get the last laugh, though, declaring to the camera: "They can laugh at me all they want. Because two more years until I retire with full benefits and pension. And my wife and I, we have bought a little cottage on a lake. And I am going to get myself a stack of mystery novels, a box of cigars, and I am going to sit back and enjoy my life."

This is where the on-screen and off-screen Jerry converge, in the same way that Tom's supreme confidence in the office contrasts the insecurity he has in his relationship with his fake wife, Wendy. The idea of Jerry's off-screen persona—rendered by a wife, charming kids, vacations in Muncie, and future plans for living large and blissfully—is what charges the series with nuance and warmth. It makes Jerry not so much the butt of the joke as in on it, much like *The Office* did with their side characters Phyllis and Kevin.

"Park Safety" was a major stepping stone to finding my groove and comfort during the second season. The monologues we spoke directly to the camera were especially useful in fleshing out our characters. Not that I enjoyed them.

In "Hunting Trip," Jerry reveals his home life, and in "Park Safety," Jerry talks about his retirement plans. These monologues seem innocuous enough, but when I look back on them, they were *scary as hell*. Yes, they gave me more face time with the audience. Yes, they propped up elements of my character's backstory. And yes, they provided brief interludes, and reactions, to the plot, which also gave viewers the chance to breathe. But they also depended on a great trust between the actor, the camera operator, and the episode's director. In other words, everyone was watching me. Remember when I told you about Greg Daniels's improvisational game where Leslie walked around the set and asked each cast member about items on their desk? Talking heads required the same amount of vulnerability and improvisational technique. We were reciting lines from the script, but we were also free (and encouraged) to add flourishes as we saw fit. We called these "fun runs."

Early on in filming, Retta told me that being asked to do a talking head felt like going to the electric chair. She coped by talking as fast as possible . . . and in a Southern accent! Can you imagine? She'd become an entirely different character. During one of these early fun runs, she was so nervous that she called Leslie Donna by mistake. After she did this a few times, Greg Daniels had to interrupt. "*You're Donna*," he said. Her discomfort didn't end there. After filming for the talking head ended and the cast and crew were walking off set, Retta continued to speak in a Southern accent. Greg said, "You can talk in a normal voice again. I mean, if you want." When it came time to film, she did indeed revert to her normal speaking voice.

Greg now tells me: "That's something you want to intervene on. You want to let an actor run with a choice, but you have to intervene quick. Before it's too late." This is Greg to a T: supportive of an actor's process but also self-determined enough to step in when that process feels wrong. Retta's "Southern accent" was, plainly put, wrong.

Paul Schneider had an influence on Daniels's decision to employ talking heads. When Paul first met Greg, he told him about a Lars von Trier movie in which a character was being interviewed, as shown through the two cameras filming it. Daniels wanted *Parks* to have some of this effect, while also ensuring that it felt different from *The Office*.

Greg Daniels

I wanted to make it more colorful. Less dreary. We were trying to adjust during the first season. We didn't see the cut of the pilot until episode 3 because we were just rolling, and we thought that we had to make some adjustments. One of those was "more exteriors, fewer interiors." This is about parks, about hanging out in them. So, I begged for another day to shoot a bunch of cold opens and to be outdoors. Like the one with Jerry and Leslie and poison ivy.

The one with Jerry and Leslie and poison ivy from the first season was the one that freaked me out. Earlier in the day I'd received a call telling me I'd be doing an "improv scene outdoors with Amy," before being told what time to arrive. That was all I had to go on. I couldn't relax in the hours leading up to it, and certainly not when I arrived on location, because Amy was doing her thing and Greg was letting Amy do her thing, which, if you've seen an expert comedian performing, is a wonder to behold. Perhaps it goes without saying, but Amy was a pro at fun runs. If it wasn't her training at Second City and UCB, it was her years on *SNL* performing in front of a live studio audience—the most intimidating thing in the world because there are millions of people watching you back at home. Though I felt relaxed—like, really relaxed. After we shot the scenes, Morgan Sackett told someone, who told me, "Jim's going to work out just fine."

Morgan Sackett and Me

MORGAN: That day was hilarious!

ME: It was terrifying . . . for me. I was with Amy Poehler, the queen.

MORGAN: And Aziz was there.

ME: Yep, Aziz was there. And Amy's the queen of improv and I'm feeling like this is make-or-break.

MORGAN: I remember that being really fun. We were shooting "Rock Show," which Mike was directing. *The Office* had straight comedy cold openers. Maybe later on they were more tied to story, but they were truly nonstory comedy cold opens. We were cutting this sixth episode and Greg goes, "Our cold opens aren't funny enough," and the entire room just writes like six of them. So Mike was shooting at the show where "Rock Show" was and Amy is on a date [with Ron Perkins]. The question then was, "Where can we shoot all of these?"

ME: We were on a walking path by a creek . . .

MORGAN: Didn't you get poison ivy or something? And the kids were throwing poop bags!

ME: Haha, yes!

MORGAN: We didn't use everything we had shot, but we used yours. And yeah, I remember thinking, *This guy can hang.*

Anything went during these fun runs. We knew most of the stuff we ad-libbed wouldn't make it in, but that was the point.

Retta told me that one of her proudest moments at *Parks* was when director Dan Goor (also one of the most brilliant writers out there) told her that she had put "the button on that scene," to which she asked what in the world he was referring to. This was during season 4's episode "Campaign Shake-Up," where Donna is asked what she thinks about the water fountain and improvises the line "Do I look like I drink water?" That was the button Dan needed. Retta didn't remember improvising that line, nor did she remember dousing me with a hose. "Literally you have a hose," I recently reminded her. "And dumbass Jerry gets soaked. You were having so much fun."

Pratt was also incredibly comfortable. If you let Pratt do Pratt (a mix of bizarre physical comedy and goofiness), then Pratt shines. I think frequently of the opening to the movie *Guardians of the Galaxy*. That's Pratt at his best. There are a thousand muscles in his head that convert to comedic timing. It's a magical quality that he naturally exudes.

Chris Pratt

I always like the physical stuff, the stunts where I wanted to damage stuff. I remember, I think it was during the "Greg Pikitis" episode [season 2, episode 7]—you have to remember, the show was always on the bubble, it felt like we were fighting for our jobs—that my friend just told me, "You just have to go in there and start breaking shit. People love to see stuff get broken. If you're going to get canceled, just go down swinging." So I was like, *All right, I'm going to go do it.* On that episode, I took a glass, smashed it on the wall, it broke a sign . . . and the kid who played Greg Pikitis, he kind of broke and laughed, which was on camera . . . and then I started just making shit up, and it ended up being funny and it made the episode. From that point on, it gave me permission to just destroy shit. I went through so many props—I was breaking computers, I'd put a huge dent in a car. I just did the craziest stuff. It reminded me of that show *Double Dare*, from when I was a kid. I would just go to work and smash stuff. There were times where it was like, "Props can't fix that, electrical has to come in . . ."

Viewers take lines for granted when they're watching a show—as they should, because it's an actor's job to deliver them seamlessly and authentically—but these lines are pored over, rehearsed, reworked, and redelivered ad nauseam. Well, except if you're Aziz.

Aziz is as natural a comedic actor as anyone I've seen, and without the formal training that I and other actors have attained over decades. If you recall, Aziz began as a stand-up comic, telling jokes about his nephew Darwish's obsession with the rapper formerly known as Kanye West. When Aziz arrived on *Parks* and I witnessed him in action for the first time, I was won over by his effortless charm. To this day, every time I watch "Park Safety," I picture him squealing "In Muncie!" Aziz was relaxed on set, maybe *too* relaxed, and it bugged the crap out of Paul Schneider.

Paul's professionalism was a contrast to Aziz's casual approach. There were no arguments or anything like that, but the two of them seemed to be on opposite sides of the spectrum when it came to acting methodology. Where Paul was diligent about reading scripts and rehearsing lines to see which tone would click—spending hours on his scenes the night before— Aziz was typically laid-back. When we would do a blocking rehearsal for a scene, Aziz didn't seem to have a grasp on his lines whatsoever. Come time to film, Aziz had not only committed them to memory but delivered them with the flair that the viewer sees as Tom Haverford.

"How the heck does Aziz do it?" Paul asked me one day. "I work on these all day, and Aziz just shows up and gets it right?" Paul's vexation was less personal than it was professional, and it said more about him than it did Aziz. It wasn't his fault, or anyone else's, that Aziz was unnaturally *natural* in his approach. Every actor has their own way; it's one of the insights I've gained over my thirty years working on a wide array of shows and movies. Paul's and Aziz's styles are unique to them; there's no right way or wrong.

By mid–second season, Paul knew his days at *Parks* were dwindling. I don't wish to speak for Paul or anybody else, but things must've been strange by this point. Not only had his character arc been reduced (hitting a painful low, perhaps, in episode 22, "Telethon," where Leslie tried to persuade him not to propose to Ann since Ann didn't think he was the one, thus diminishing Mark's potential as a love interest), but he still had to meet all the expectations for an actor despite knowing his time on the show was nearing the end.

Mike had called the cast into a meeting to tell us this sad news and reassured us that Paul was going to be okay, that he had work lined up for a new Woody Allen film. Paul's walking away from the show was "mutual," Mike said. Given my relationship with Paul, we had a lot of heart-to-hearts in the waning weeks of season 2, which allowed me to be there for my friend. I hope he felt better because of that, too.

This was a weird time, though. It's hard to say what was in

Paul's head, but that lightness he'd previously carried around seemed zapped out of him, and he appeared tired and withdrawn. He didn't stay around set if he didn't have to, and in between shooting and catching him between scenes, I tried to be jovial and lighthearted about everything. It was a tough situation and we all did the best we could.

Still, Paul was a professional, and even though he and I never directly addressed the elephant in the room that was his impending departure, he remained a friend to me through his last day on set. We haven't stayed as close over the years, but before he left, I threw a party for him at my house. What better way to send him off than as friends enjoying barbecue and beers?

I did feel conflicted, though. Mike Schur had just told me and Retta the news that we'd been made series regulars. I was overjoyed. Meanwhile Paul—a regular from day one—had been reduced to a ghost of a part. It was hard to outwardly celebrate knowing my friend was moving on.

Retta

Unlike Jim, I try not to get overly excited about news like being named a series regular. I just never know if it's going to be real. For example, when I was told I would be a series regular, my manager told me two opposing things: "I have good news and bad news. The good is that they want to make you a series regular. The bad news is . . . this is what they're offering you." And then he showed me a not-so-great offer. I do remember when Mike first told us, though. I guess my instinct was that, *Well, cool, but we've also been here for a couple of seasons*, so I don't know if it changed much.

Another major change was the arrival of Adam Scott and Rob freaking Lowe. There was no reason given, by Mike or anyone else, for Adam and Rob joining the cast by the end of season 2, but it doesn't take a genius to figure out the contributions they could bring. Though I didn't know Adam Scott personally, I was a fan of his work on *Party Down*, one of my favorite shows. I was excited to work with him professionally and observe the lighthearted sensitivity that he brought to his character. Adam Scott's Ben was, in my eyes, a counter to the raging hormones of Ron and Tom, not to mention a suitable love interest for Leslie. In a big ironic twist, I also found out that Adam had auditioned for the role of Mark Brendanawicz and hadn't gotten it. Maybe things happen for a reason after all.

Adam Scott, *Ben Wyatt*

I was a big fan of the show, an avid watcher of it, so getting the call was super weird and incredibly exciting. I was doing *Party Down* at the time and we'd just finished shooting season 2 and were waiting to see if we'd get picked up for season 3 . . . and it wasn't looking good. It seemed like it probably wasn't going to happen. And Mike [Schur] had heard about that likelihood out in the ether, so he, being a fan of *Party Down*, called me in for a meeting where we just chatted for a while. I got to meet a lot of the writers as well. Mike is an incredibly easy person to get along with.

Then it was a matter of deciding whether to do *Parks*, which was . . . the easiest decision in the world. The only thing was *Party Down* wasn't officially canceled yet, so I was in a tough place where we all knew it was going to be canceled, but it not being official and me taking another job was really hard on me. I remember talking to a contact at Starz at the time who was very high up and who indeed let me know that it was going to be canceled and that, yeah, I could take this job. I *should* take the job.

I auditioned for Mark originally, but it was just a "side character" at that point because the pilot hadn't even been written. One of my auditions was with Rashida. Nick was there, too, I believe. I remember hearing about this "*Office* spin-off" for a while, and I think it was a year before I actually auditioned that I told my agent that I wanted to be part of it.

I was very nervous when I showed up for the first table read. I remember driving in and parking, and right when I was in that parking garage that was adjacent to our stage there, I remember thinking, *Oh, I don't have very much time and I still have to walk over to that building, get into that elevator,* etc. I had timed it so that I'd be five minutes early, but now I realize that I'm going to show up exactly on time. This was a *big* mistake because I walk in and everyone's seated and the room is packed with people, which compounded my nervousness. But as far as table reads go, it was a welcoming room and had such a responsive atmosphere. I remember at the end of the table read I breathed an audible sigh of relief. Aubrey came up to me and passed me a note that was folded up very tight— do you remember the movie *Shutter Island* where Leonardo DiCaprio and Mark Ruffalo go to the mental hospital, and I think someone passes them a note? At the time it was a famous moment that had just happened in a famous movie—and Aubrey's note said "Run," just like in the movie. It was a perfect welcome note.

Greg Daniels

The biggest change at *Parks* was the addition of Adam and Rob once Paul left. That was the biggest news shock then. Paul's role was sort of to be this love interest for Amy [Leslie], but I don't think there was any chemistry there, so that just wasn't really going anywhere.

When we were casting for Mark, it was down to Paul and Chris O'Dowd, and sometimes I wonder what it would've been like if we'd gone with Chris. To me, Paul was a very good actor, but he didn't start out as an actor; he started out as an editor or cinematographer. He was a super-handsome guy who didn't have the personality of a super-handsome guy. He had this introverted, oddball personality, and he didn't grow into what we thought we were going to grow into.

Adam auditioned for the role of Mark. He also auditioned for the Jim Halpert role [in *The Office*] back in the day. At that time, I thought of him as too close to the Jim Halpert character because he had auditioned for it. And Rob . . . the funny thing about the Rob thing is . . . in retrospect, it was such a great thing for the show, but were Adam and Rob too close to each other? Two handsome guys, you know? So, we met with Rob Lowe and he told us this story—he's such a storyteller—about Tom Cruise taking vitamins, and that's essentially Chris Traeger.* You're always scared to make a choice, but this turned out to be a great choice.

---

* I have no clue what the Tom Cruise story is, but if his vitamin regimen is anything like Chris Traeger's . . . a lot of things are starting to make sense.

Seeing Rob Lowe walk on set for his first table read was unreal. Rob is only a couple years younger than me—I know, I know, we look so much alike. He was at the center of some of the biggest films of the '80s and series of the '00s, in addition to pop culture in general—Sam Seaborn, Billy Hicks, Sodapop, Number 2.

To state the obvious, Rob was charming during his first table read—how could he not be? He looked people in the eye, joked around, and made this jarring transition feel less jarring. He might have overshadowed Adam a little bit, but it's hard to steal focus from Rob. He is, after all, Rob freaking Lowe.

My confusion around Paul leaving and Adam and Rob joining wouldn't abate for some time, but if I'd died that season, I would've been happy knowing I'd been in the same room as Rob Lowe. One of the reasons he was brought on, besides Mike Schur being a giant fan of *The West Wing*, was how he could bring a new fan base to the show, one slightly older than the millennials who watched *The Office*. Rob's energy and persona were a sharp contrast to Paul's, and many were excited about this evolution (including me, although, as I said earlier, with some reluctance). But the signing-on of Rob Lowe *and* Adam Scott also meant there would be two screen-filling acting spots where there previously was one, and I'd be lying if I said that I didn't worry about how that would affect me and my standing. If getting to know Pratt and Paul had taught me anything—and I believe it taught me a lot!—it's that people are capable of some amazing surprises.

Snapped a pic of some of the boys on set.

We're
Not
Gonna
Take It

The excitement about Rob Lowe hit a fever pitch when we screened season 3, episode 2, "Flu Season." Although we hadn't done many screenings up to this point, and wouldn't do many others following it, the producers must have thought a public screening with Rob would help generate more publicity about the show. This is the episode where Rob Lowe's Chris Traeger catches the flu and his perfect "microchipped" body is "compromised," which delights Ann Perkins because, in her eyes, it makes him normal. Well, as normal as someone like Chris Traeger can be. "The problem is he's like a perfect human man," Ann says during one talking head. "I can't find one flaw." Well, neither could the audience at the screening, who oohed and ahhed every time Rob entered the frame. They're not wrong—he's physically perfect . . . even when he "can't stop pooping."

This little show that could was gathering more momentum, with the positive talk among critics, at screening parties, and at random events across America. Despite our mounting success as a collective, people just couldn't get enough of Rob. Years later, when we took a trip to Indianapolis to film with the Colts (season 5, episode 10), I was surprised to see that the excitement for him hadn't waned a bit. Fans gawked at him as he made his way down the plane aisle, second only to the enthusiasm they showed me. Kidding!

I'm reminded of the time I went out to dinner at Filomena Ristorante in Washington, DC, with several of *The Office*'s alumni, including Kate Flannery (Meredith) and Oscar Nuñez (Oscar). We were greeted by the host on a particularly busy Saturday night. "It's gonna be, uh, at least two hours," the host said apologetically.

We're sporting sour faces because this was Rob's last day on set. (Chris and Ann were heading to Michigan.) It was a tough day.

The night of "The Fight," where things got a li'l out of hand.

Me, Oscar Nuñez, and Kate Flannery enjoying a meal in Georgetown. Minds blown! Parks officially meets The Office.

"No problem, we'll come back," I said. Just as we were turning around to find space at the bar, we heard a scream. It turns out that another patron who was also waiting for a table had recognized us. Her mind was blown.

"I'm so sorry," she said, embarrassed. "It's just . . . *The Office. Parks and Rec.* You guys . . . together . . . how? I mean, like, oh my goodness!" Her scream had gotten the attention of some of the other restaurant employees, who also recognized us. And wouldn't you know it, we got a table. As a matter of fact, they had to move us to a private dining area because we were creating a bit of a disturbance for the other diners. Never underestimate the power of a character actor.

Now, back to season 3, which was thrilling for me on many levels, as a viewer and as an actor. It introduced Ben and Leslie's relationship (episode 14, "Road Trip"); Jerry's painting was the center of episode 11's "Jerry's Painting"—hats off to whatever genius painted Aziz's cherub for that episode; and we got one of the greatest TV songs ever by way of Mouse Rat's "5,000 Candles in the Wind." Not to mention "Harvest Festival" (episode 7), in which Jerry gets lost in a corn maze and his brethren do little in the way of finding him. Perhaps most memorable of all was "The Fight," where we all get drunk off of our asses. While filming it, we each got to play in front of the camera and do our best drunk impressions, and Amy, ever a fan of improv, let us riff and do whatever the hell we wanted. This applied to the end of the episode, too, when Jerry gets strapped to the top of a car and driven away. Because the crew was always concerned about our safety, they tried to push a stunt double on me, but I ultimately declined . . . and they ultimately relented. The Jerry you see in the final shot is me. What other job lets you get tied to the top of a car and driven away?

Adam Scott

I connected with Ben from the very start. The circumstance of the character, his backstory of him being this kid mayor who really does have ambition in politics and public service and is gifted in politics and public service but had this tough beginning that he's ashamed of. Humiliated by. It's so great for an actor to have that kind of backstory.

I watched "The Master Plan" [season 2, episode 23] when it was on TV recently, and that first scene where Amy and I sit down to talk at the bar is terrific. It was like that back then, when there was this ease and connection between me and Amy. It just felt right. And these characters needed each other and had no idea how much, but they fit together like puzzle pieces almost immediately even though they don't face up to it for a while. Ben is able to see right into Leslie's ambition, and Leslie connects with Ben being this child mayor. It reminds her of being a young girl.

I was quite nervous during my first few episodes on *Parks* getting on my feet, but when you're working with Amy you're immediately put at ease. There's an immediate connection to her and to the material.

We were doing a lot of traveling over the course of season 3, too. Not only did some of the episodes call for on-location spots (Leslie goes to Indianapolis in the season opener, and she and

Ben return to Pawnee in episode 14), but we were making the rounds on the numerous late-night shows. The most extraordinary among these visits was to *The Tonight Show Starring Jimmy Fallon*, where Jimmy and the Roots joined forces with our entire cast to compete in an epic singing battle in the style of a *Glee* sectional, complete with green sweat suits and a healthy rivalry between the *Parks* crew and Fallon's "group."

Amy had asked us if we wanted to do it a couple weeks earlier. It was Twisted Sister's "We're Not Gonna Take It," she told us, which is all she needed to say. It's a badass song.

It's worth mentioning that this was one of those times when Amy was telling the cast about the offer, and it was just not clicking for me that I was *part* of the invite.

"Wait, you mean me and Retta, too?" I asked Amy in front of the group.

"Jim, of course!" she said. "You, Retta, everyone."

The Fox show *Glee* was all the rage at the time, so Jimmy, with his love of karaoke contests and his wheel of musical impressions, thought our ensemble cast would be a great complement to his hilarious antics. Jimmy's also a terrific human: years after the *Parks* cast performed on his show, he and I ran into each other in Los Angeles at some NBC event, where he recognized me immediately and pulled me into a warm embrace. Jimmy Fallon is a bit of a phenomenon—an actor (who breaks character a lot; check out his adorable *SNL* days), singer, dancer, and wonderful interviewer on top of all that. The fact that he's also a down-to-earth guy is icing on the cake.

The *Fallon* crew took care of us: I'm talking limo rides to and from the airport and hotel, first-class airfare, lavish hotels, catered meals. Although I'm not someone who yearns for top-notch amenities, it's nice to be surprised by them. Truly, is there anything better than sitting with Chris Pratt and Anna Faris in a hotel lobby bar and getting to ask Anna all your questions about the *Scary Movie* franchise?

Anna and I first met when we guested on an episode of *Friends* during its final season (she was recurring), and we bonded based on being guest stars on a show that featured a tight-knit group. (Sound familiar?) While the cast was welcoming, we were the "outsiders" who would walk to our cars together and talk about what went on during rehearsal and how exciting it was to be guesting on *Friends*. We were both grateful to the cast for being so welcoming.

On the <u>Tonight Show</u> set, shooting the <u>Glee</u> parody.

It wasn't all R & R for *Fallon* in NYC. For two days, from morning until evening, we rehearsed religiously to get every note and step of the performance just right. For left-feeters like me, Pratt, and Nick, the work felt insurmountable at times . . . even if I looked swanky in my Irish cap. On top of all that work, Amy was *very* pregnant and a trooper at every turn. If we had to retry some choreography, she did it. She even had friends from *SNL* play for Fallon's team—one of them being Paula Pell, who would star as Tamara Swanson, Ron's mother (aka "the OG Tammy"). She's one of the funniest and wittiest people I've ever met.

Rashida, I learned, follows in her father Quincy Jones's footsteps when it comes to singing and musicality; she's even recorded songs and music videos. Amy is no slouch either.

Me? I needed all the help I could get. Amy, Rashida, and Retta were nailing it, but I would say the guys . . . not so much. But it didn't matter. That joy and passion that you see on each of our faces on *Fallon* is as pure as anything I've experienced, and it gave fans a small glimpse into our working styles.

You see, being on set all day is exhausting—whether it's blocking out several scenes or doing take after take until one feels right. Exhilarating, yes, but also exhausting. My "day in the life" began with my call time, the time I was required to show up on set. Once there, I'd head to hair and makeup, which the guys had a much easier time with than the girls. The call times were tricky and varied for everyone, since they were dependent on who was needed for each scene. Some days I had a 7 a.m. call time, other days late morning or afternoon, or even evenings if that was the only scene I had to shoot that day. Once we were ready to work, we'd read the scene out loud before starting to block it. Then we'd put it on its feet and see what felt right. Once the director and actors were happy with it, they'd call for the crew to come in to watch and take an inventory of what would be needed for lighting, sound, and camera angles. After they were prepared, the "second team," or "stand-ins," would come in and take over for us actors while we changed into wardrobe or finished with hair and makeup. If there was downtime after that,

I'd hang in someone's trailer (usually Retta's) or go back to my own and watch TV, read, or prepare for an audition if I had one lined up. Sooner or later, we'd be called to set to shoot the scene.

When the show first started, it was a Monday–Friday shooting schedule, and the hours could be anywhere between 7 a.m. and midnight. As the years went on and the show became a well-oiled machine, most of our days wouldn't be longer than ten hours. It also would depend on location shooting. We shot outside of the soundstage about two days a week (sometimes more/sometimes less). As opposed to the soundstage, which you could control, shooting on location contained variables that could ruin or delay a shoot. Planes flying overhead. Cars not adhering to road detours. Construction noise from blocks away. It can be incredibly frustrating, especially if a take gets blown because of outside factors. That said, it's the nature of the biz.

So there you have it—a mix of monotony and repetition, day after day, that is sweetened by snack breaks and hang sessions in between. And sometimes by epic dance sessions in the hair-and-makeup trailers.

You didn't misread that. Epic dance sessions in the hair-and-makeup trailers.

Amy must have originated these sessions since she spent so much time in the trailers. Either she, Rashida, or Autumn, the head of the makeup department, would put on a song like "Work Out" by J. Cole, start dancing, and encourage the rest of the cast to follow suit. The ladies were all talented dancers who'd put us boys to shame, but, unlike the "contest" on *Fallon*, there were no choreographed moves or expectations. Just spontaneity in the name of some good old-fashioned fun. To this day, a group chat exists between several of the cast members (we call it the Parks

Family Text) where these videos are occasionally shared to remind us of our dancing days. It's hard not to laugh each time.
Retta—the so-called Queen of Memories—finds the best ones to
embarrass us with.

At some point during filming for season 3, I got my first official invitation to Rashida's birthday party, a pajama-and-candy-
themed event that she hosted each year at her father's house. By
"her father," I mean music legend Quincy Jones.

The only "rule" of Rashida's party was that you had to show
up in pajamas. I hadn't bought pajamas in years, since my mom
bought me a pair for Christmas when I was in my twenties.
(What is it with moms and pajamas?) So I purchased a $75
set—expensive as hell, yeah, but did I wear them to Rashida's
party the next year, too? And the year after that? Course I did.
Rashida was serious about her pajama party: stories had circulated about people—famous ones—getting turned away because
they hadn't shown up wearing them.

I was greeted by a valet and escorted into a house decorated
with every type of candy you can imagine. Decking the halls
were Ding Dongs, Ho Hos, candy canes, Skittles, Mounds, and
chocolate-covered raisins from foreign countries with names
spelled out in languages I couldn't make out. In addition to the
overabundance of candy, every celebrity was there: I'm not going to name-drop because I'm humbler than that, but seeing
Chris Pine in pajamas? Paul Rudd? Mind blown. Still, since I

was older than Rashida and her super-cool peers, I was more excited to see Quincy Jones or Rashida's other famous parent, Peggy Lipton (*The award for most talented family goes to . . .*), than to meet any of the hip DJs who were busy spinning records and whose stage names I couldn't phonetically pronounce.

My meeting Quincy wasn't intentional, believe me. I'm not some stalker. The last thing I'd ever do is attend Rashida's party, thank her for the invite, and inquire as to where I could find her dad. Even though this was Quincy's house, his privacy was to be respected. Otherwise, I could've kissed away those $75 pajamas. I wouldn't need them again.

Being the curious person I am, I escaped the dancing portion of the evening and wandered into a room that doubled as a museum of awards and accolades. Grammys, framed platinum records, photos of Michael Jackson, Sarah Vaughan, Peggy Lee, Oprah, and Sinatra. Memorabilia from 1985's "We Are the World," in which Bob Dylan's halfhearted performance has become the stuff that GIFs are made of. I had entered a hall of fame representing Quincy Jones's marvelous career and had managed not to touch a thing (I swear).

I had no idea if Quincy was in the house, but I kept my eyes and ears peeled and soon heard a voice coming from the adjacent kitchen. It was familiar and induced both excitement and terror: excitement because I knew the voice belonged to Quincy, and terror because I was a mere few feet from him! I sauntered into the kitchen to find Quincy (who was not sporting pajamas) sitting there with his friend, trying to enjoy a private conversation in the sanctity of his own home. That is, until I ruined it.

The room fell silent. I stared. Quincy and his friend stared back. A caterer, who was alternating between cleaning surfaces and arranging treats on a plate, stopped in her tracks. I realized at that instant that I was being a total intruder. (I would say stalker but maybe that's too strong . . . maybe.)

"Uhhh, hi," I finally uttered.

"Hi," Quincy replied.

I was trying hard to say something, to say anything to cut the silence, and so out it came: "Uh, yeah, I'm Jim. I work with your daughter."

"I know you do," he said.

Now he was smiling. A laugh seeped out. I was smiling, too, but out of overwhelming embarrassment. Somewhere in the absurdity of my mind, I had neglected to understand that, as Rashida's father, he most likely watched *Parks* to see his daughter's performance week after week. If he didn't know my name (and why should he?), he at least recognized me from the show.

It was also a huge thrill to briefly get to meet her mother, Peggy Lipton (who did sport pajamas), around whom I didn't embarrass myself and perhaps even redeemed myself with some conversation about 1970s television. Peggy has since passed away, and I know that was such a big loss to Rashida and her family. It's easy to see where Rashida's beauty comes from, inside and out.

Amy, Rashida, and Aubrey had become a family of their own. As the youngest star of the show, Aubrey had been welcomed by Amy and Rashida as soon as she began work. Aubrey had worked as a page at *SNL*, where she reportedly shared fake facts on the tours she gave while sneaking off to privately dispel her hangover. She'd rise through the ranks of the comedy/improv world and become a familiar face at UCB, which might've been how Amy first heard about her, but her entry into *Parks* was due to Allison Jones's casting call. Rewatching *Parks* all these years later, I'm stunned at the role that Aubrey's character April plays in so many plotlines and individual scenes: she complements Andy's goofiness with a deadpan version of her own, and she softens Ron's masculinity by way of her adorable independence. While credit goes to the show's writers for making April Ludgate such a quirky character, it was Aubrey herself who made the character unique. Mike Schur has said in multiple interviews that April was written into the show based on his and Alison Jones's reaction to Aubrey's audition, where he felt like he'd met one of the weirdest people of his life. How I feel about Ron Swanson is also how I feel about April Ludgate: only one person in the world could've played that role.

Allison Jones

I love how Mike has said he was kind of afraid of her and still is. LOL. She was one of a kind and stared a lot and didn't say much and had a compelling anti-actor quality to her. Mike and Greg are two of the few writer-producers ever willing to see someone without a role in mind.

Aubrey was barely twenty-five when *Parks* began—though not a kid, she was much younger than me, Nick, and Amy. While we wouldn't try to shield her young mind from our bawdy humor (she was as much a jokester as we were), we checked in with her to make sure she was comfortable on and off of set. Amy and

Rashida, as entertainment icons and powerful feminist leaders, did a lot of the heavy lifting to bring Aubrey into the fold, from visiting her in her trailer to arranging after-shoot hangs to acting as lifelines for anything that Aubrey needed while filming. I'm sure that it meant a lot to Aubrey's family knowing that she had mentors like Amy and Rashida.

In 2013, Aubrey invited me to a screening of *The To Do List*, a movie she'd filmed with Bill Hader, Johnny Simmons, Adam Pally, Donald Glover, and others. I sat next to Aubrey's father, David, who's around my age, and we watched this coming-of-age film about a girl going off to college. In this case, she is sexually inexperienced and wants to complete everything on her sex "to-do list" before leaving. I squirmed in my seat as Aubrey's character did some, shall we say, "dirty things" in the movie. After the screening, I tried to defuse her father's discomfort by introducing some boring small talk in the lobby, and maybe, just maybe, I was expressing protectiveness of Aubrey by trying to make her father feel better. In reality, I probably felt more awkward than he did. For the record, Aubrey doesn't need protecting from anyone or anything: she's one of the bravest, funniest, and most ambitious people I know.

Amy continued to set the tone throughout season 3. Though pregnant with her second child by the time we were filming, she was also always the first one on set and in hair and makeup at five thirty in the morning. If she ever had morning sickness or headaches, she never showed it. Every morning, I'd arrive and ask Amy how she was feeling. As vivaciously as ever came her reply: "I'm great, buddy. How are you?!"

As critical praise for *Parks* grew (our ratings not so much), we had lots of interested people knocking on our doors, from actors

Amy and Aubrey between scenes at Lucas Oil Stadium in Indianapolis.

who wanted to do guest spots, like Nick Kroll, to directors who wanted to get in on the fun. Whenever a guest director came aboard to film an episode, the producers would go around to the regular cast and crew and ask how things were going. They wanted to make sure that we always felt heard. If a director's style wasn't making us comfortable, the producers would take care of it. It's true that when filming a sitcom, you simply must "get the work done," but, usually, the only people we'd hear yelling were the assistant directors who were tasked with keeping us on schedule, which, in turn, kept us on budget. That was really the only time you'd hear loud squawks and squeals and not feel bad about your performance. If you were a guest director screaming to inflate your ego and impress upon the set your "inimitable" vision, then you were just acting like a jerk.

I've met every kind of director there is—the reserved type, the inquisitive kind, the screamer, the laugher. We weeded out the types who prided themselves on power and "always being right." If a director wasn't fair and collaborative, they wouldn't be invited back to the *Parks* set.

I can't speak for the other actors, but I was always bothered when a guest director would make demands of a character by trying to convince you that following their direction for your character was the only thing that could make the scene function well. Rather than give suggestions, for instance, these kinds of directors were on a quest to rewrite the show in their own heads, or to persuade you that your choices were wrong and theirs right. The thing is, I know Jerry/Garry/Terry/Larry/Barry better than any director, just as Pratt knows Andy and Nick knows Ron.

I'll give you an example. At the end of 2022, I traveled to

Memphis, Tennessee, to do a guest spot on *Young Rock*. After half a day of shooting, the director sauntered over to me and said, "This is so good, you have such a wide range. And you can take all the notes." And he was right: as a guest actor, I'll take *all the notes in the world*. That's because the character is new and the chances of returning to set scarce. But when you're on a show for a while, notes become less helpful. You're immersed in the character's biography. Hell, you've even invented some of their biography along the way.

It's no one's fault. Actor, director, line producer, cinematographer—they're all trying to do what's right for a given shot, and for the episode. In my experience, no one is as diligent in this regard as James Spader.

A few years before *Parks* kicked off, I did an episode of *Boston Legal*, starring James Spader and William Shatner, in which my guest character, Gil Furnald, is fired from his post as Santa at a department store after it's revealed that he enjoys wearing women's clothing. In some parts of the country today, this might not be seen as a progressive, boundary-pushing plot, but in 2004 it wasn't far off. It seemed to me that William Shatner himself wasn't okay with this. Nor was his character. In one scene, when Gil Furnald tells Shatner's Denny Crane his reasoning behind dressing up as a woman ("It's not a sexual turn-on. It . . . well . . . it just feels right sometimes"), Denny Crane responds, "So, basically you're a sicko?" The writers of this episode were attempting to pry into the expectations that society places on those who don't adhere to "normal" ways, whatever that word means, but off-screen, it appeared that William Shatner might have been falling victim to the very thing the show's writers were exposing. Whenever my character wore a dress or earrings, Shatner appeared to be aloof, sometimes even cold, to me. He kept scanning me up and down, his floppy smile transformed. Was it disgust? At one point between takes, he said to Spader, "Thank God, this is yours," seemingly glad that Spader's character, and not his, would be legally representing Gil in this episode. I don't know if Shatner was joking, or maybe he's a Method actor, or maybe I was just overly sensitive. Whatever it was, it definitely made me uncomfortable. It was already weird enough having to show up to set on my first day in a dress and high heels in front of the cast and crew.

There's a heartfelt scene toward the end of the episode where my Gil and Spader's Alan Shore are sitting in a bar. I should say that this was one of the last scenes we shot after a grueling ten-day schedule. As it was, we were already behind. But now, we had a big scene to shoot—perhaps the biggest scene—and we were again running late. By the time the cameras were ready to roll, it was "golden time," which refers to work that goes beyond the planned shooting schedule, at which point cast and crew need to be paid extra. Adding to the anxiety permeating the room was the fact that the scene centers on Gil and Shore sharing a personal, reflective conversation; the tone had to be just right. If it wasn't, the episode would fall apart. In the scene, Gil explains how tough life has been because of his being both gay and a cross-dresser.

We began with the usual wide-shot coverage of the scene and then moved in to tighter over-the-shoulder shots on each of the actors. After we got Spader's coverage, it was my turn. We were fighting the clock and I could feel the rushed atmosphere from the set. Everybody wanted to go home, and I totally understand why. The crew had already put in twelve to fourteen hours. I didn't blame them for wanting to be done.

We did the first take, which was okay. Not great . . . but okay. I knew I could do better. After the second take, the director said, "Great. What do you guys think?" I took that as his saying that it was good enough and that we could wrap this thing up. I knew I wasn't fully content with my performance, but I also knew that everybody wanted out. Plus, I was only a guest star. Why would they do another take *just for me*?

But this was Spader's show, and nobody moved on until he was happy. The director said, "That was good, guys, very good . . . James, you happy?" A key grip was preparing to break the lighting down. Spader looked at me, then leaned in tight. "What do you think, Jim? Were you happy with that take?"

"It was okay," I said. I couldn't lie to James Spader. Dude is so intense, in the best way.

"Wanna do it again?"

"I would, but we're kinda under the gun here, no?" The director heard me say this; his eyes widened. *Yes, yes, yes we are,* they told me. *Yes, yes, yes,* the ADs visually mouthed. *Under the gun, yes. Good enough!*

Spader must've had eyes behind his head, because he turned to the director and, without hesitation, said: "Respectfully, we're going to do this again. And then again. And then maybe another time after that."

Dayum.

The director snapped awake. The crew got into place. Action was called.

We did a take, and then two more. After the third, Spader and I both knew we had nailed it. He said, "I think that was it. What do you think?"

"Hell yeah," I said. "That was the one."

Actors know when we connect and magic occurs. You get lost in the moment. When my character explained to Spader's what his life had been like, I could feel the intensity in my bones. We both could. That connectedness is the mental drug that keeps actors acting and won't let us stop. Spader had taught me one of the most important lessons of my career, too: a show is nothing without its actors, and its actors need to be happy with their performances. A talented director, even with a marvelous script, can help an actor get there, but they can't make them cross the finish line.

After we wrapped, Spader and I talked about vineyards in Napa as we headed back to our trailers. Turns out the man knows his wine. I remember thinking that it was a perfect day, made so because of my costar's commitment to near perfection.

Which brings me back to *Parks*. Not everything on a show is perfect, and with Rob Lowe, there came baggage. I'm not talking about the heavy, need-five-people-to-carry-it type of baggage. Nor do I mean emotional. I simply mean that if you're Rob freaking Lowe, you have a reputation that precedes you. And, if you recall, the acting world is like the middle school cafeteria— where reputations fester on lunch trays.

By the time Rob began work with us in earnest, the cast had been together for nearly two years and had developed a well-oiled system for filming scenes and achieving good results. We'd show up on set, scripts in hand. We would read the scene out loud and then block it with the director, finding out where to stand or sit or how to move. Then we'd pose any questions about the scene to the director and/or writer, get answers, and run through it again for the crew so they could see how to light us and where to put the cameras and mics. Finally, we'd leave, go to wardrobe and makeup, and come back ready to shoot for real. While it sounds complicated, it's nothing when you consider the hour-long-drama format of a show like *The West Wing*, which Rob had been on for many years.

During Rob and Adam's first scene with all of us—one where Chris Traeger and his fellow newbie character, Ben Wyatt, have a conversation in the "bullpen" of the Parks Department office—we did our usual rehearsal, but at the end, Rob looked a bit concerned. He talked to the director, and I got the feeling he wanted to do things differently than we were used to, maybe rehearse more or make changes. To be honest, I'm not 100 percent sure what was on his mind.

Rob has done many shows where he's number one on the call sheet. That adds a lot of pressure, because that's the actor who sets the tone. It's good for the ego, but it comes with responsibility. This was different for him. He was joining a show that was up and running. We already had our number one in Amy, and she was perfection.

Amy walked over to Rob, and she explained to him our process, the way we'd been doing it for the past two seasons. Now, I don't want to put words or feelings into Rob's mouth, but I felt like I saw him take it all in. There was a moment of hesitation, and then the realization that "Hey, I don't have to carry this. I can just go with the flow."

Rob's face changed after that conversation. Relief shone where uncertainty once had, as if it dawned on him that he didn't have to run the show. *Parks* wasn't one of those big-time movies where so much fell upon one actor's shoulders. He was part of an ensemble, one that had been working well. To be in an ensemble, one had to fit *in*, not stand *out*. That was the Amy Poehler magic, which feels effortless and invisible and crops up when it's needed most.

And that's exactly what Rob did: he went with the flow. Throughout his run with the show, Rob was on board with the rest of us. From what I've heard him say, it was one of his most fun experiences as an actor.

Karen, Richards, and Seaborn... Oh My!

These awe-inspiring moments, like Rob Lowe walking on set, can happen to any of us. Whether you're a family member visiting a soundstage show for the first time or you're me, on set every day, it's hard not to be impressed by the characters (and actors) you've grown to love.

As a huge *Will & Grace* and Megan Mullally fanatic, maybe the hugest, I was graced by the presence of the queen herself whenever she did guest spots on *Parks*. Megan had made her debut on season 2, episode 8, "Ron and Tammy," which spurred a follow-up episode in season 3 entitled, you guessed it, "Ron & Tammy 2." By season 4, Megan's Tammy 2 would be recruited by Leslie Knope to help eradicate Tammy 1 because Leslie believes that Tammy 1 has turned Ron into a proper wimp. If only he could gain back the snarl, the type that led him to say of Tammy 2, "Tammy is a mean person. She's a grade-A bitch. Every time she laughs, an angel dies. Even telemarketers avoid her." I've always loved that line. Megan's Tammy 2 did a lot in terms of character development of Nick's Ron: She softened Ron. She made him more vulnerable—desperately so. The damage is so vast that come season 7's "Ron & Jammy," Ron and Leslie must stage an intervention for Jeremy Jamm (Jon Glaser) to try to break the spell Tammy has on him. Ron is the only person who can understand the depraved damage she's caused. He's haunted by it.

By the time we were filming season 3, Megan had become a regular around *Parks*' set because she is, of course, married to Nick. She would appear at screenings and wrap parties, which made her part of our family. That familiarity didn't stop me from geeking out whenever I'd run into her. I'd first seen her years earlier while filming an audition and was heading back to my car at the CBS Radford lot. Megan drove by me in a new Porsche gifted to her and her fellow cast members by the producers of *Will & Grace* to celebrate their success.

On the *Parks* set, it was so hard to see Megan as someone other than Karen Walker. I had to mentally check myself once or twice before addressing her as Karen.

Megan was cool, though. She's someone who played one of the most iconic characters on TV, to say nothing of her other work, and is probably asked about *Will & Grace* two hundred times a day. That didn't prevent her from addressing my occasional questions about what it was like to work with Sean Hayes and Debra Messing or do a burlesque performance in one of the episodes, though I was careful to control my fanboying, reminding myself that Megan was like any other person visiting their partner on set. She was there to be present for and encouraging of Nick . . . *but, oh my God, no way, it's Karen Walker!*

One day, I brought a friend to set because she wanted to meet Nick. I took her to Nick's trailer, and I could see my friend's anticipation building. "Are you sure he won't mind? He's probably pretty busy," she said.

I had a little fun with this one. "Well, he usually doesn't like visitors, but he likes me, so . . . worth a shot?"

"No, no, no, Jim. No way. I don't want to upset him."

"You won't be. I'm the one bringing you here. He'll probably be nice to you but yell at me. After the fact. Probably. No, most likely."

"You're joking, right?"

I knocked. My friend took two giant steps backward. I knocked again.

Coming!

That was strange, I thought. Nick sounds different.

The trailer door opened and out came Megan.

"What the fuck!"

That was my friend shouting. She had lost her cool after Megan greeted her. "What the fuck, it's Karen Walker."

At least it wasn't me who said it.

Megan smiled and gave my friend a big hug.

I have to admire Megan because any actor who has spent significant time on a sitcom or drama faces a beautiful challenge: the part for which they've garnered fame and attention can also become a burden. Both Megan and Sean have handled that burden with, um, grace.

I had my own encounters with fans. During season 3's "Indianapolis," the other episode we filmed in Indy, a lovely young woman standing in the crowd asked if she could show me some drawings. "Of course!" I replied.

Note to self: whenever somebody asks to show you drawings (plural), you know you have, shall we say, a passionate fan in your vicinity.

"I drew these," she said. "They're . . . all of you." And that they were: drawings—not exactly Picasso's but decently sketched. *A* for effort.

Happy birthday, Megan! And yes, I agree. I am number one.

She pulled out a drawing of every one of us: Amy, Nick, Rashida, Aziz, Retta, Chris, Rob, Adam, Aubrey, and me. "Oh my goodness," I bluffed, "they are . . . amazing!"

"You think?"

"Oh yes," I said.

The young woman was looking for an acknowledgment for her work and love of the show. I decided, though, to take things a step further. I decided that she needed our autographs. "What do you think?" I asked. "Do you want them signed?"

"You can do that?" she asked. She sounded as unsure as I was.

"I think I can!" I replied. "No, no, I definitely can. Give me a minute."

I took her drawings and sauntered over to the trailer where everyone was sitting. My friends burst out laughing when they saw me juggling the cardboard frames. "Oh noooooo," one of them cried, "O'Heir got sucked in!"

"No I didn't!"

"You did! Look at all that! Are those gifts? Signature requests?"

"Uhhhh . . . signature requests."

"That's a lot of signatures," someone said. "She asked you to sign *all* of those?"

"I asked her if she wanted them signed."

The room fell silent. Amy bit her lip, as if saying *Oh my God*.

"O'Heir got sucked in," they repeated. "Hahahahaha!" Aziz turned then into roastmaster Jeff Ross and I became the honorary roastee. I've watched these things on Comedy Central: some roastees don't like the jokes, but nobody dislikes being roasted. I was known as the guy who would get too involved with extras from the set. I was mercilessly teased about it, and I deserved it.

I *did* get too involved. There was an extra on the show whom I ended up helping move three different times. To quote the green witch from *Wicked*, "No good deed goes unpunished." I don't necessarily believe that, but it has come to bite me in the ass a few times.

"No, no, you don't understand," I protested to the gang back in the trailer. "They're . . . of us!" I showed them the drawings and watched as my fellow castmates, previously critical, melted a bit.

"Jim," they said, "they're perfect." *Well, not perfect, but you get the idea. The intention was perfect.* Each of us signed our portrait and wrote a little sentiment to our newly discovered fan.

I know what it's like to be a fan, and one of my idols was Mary Tyler Moore. Unfortunately, Ms. Moore did not guest on a *Parks* episode. (If she had, I would've flipped my lid.) But the great success she found in not one but two sitcoms—first *The Dick Van Dyke Show* and then the show bearing her name—proves that some people have elevated talents beyond normal comprehension. I'm not the only person who holds her in such high regard. Greg Daniels, who worked at *SNL* from 1987 to 1993, recently told me that he considers Mary Tyler Moore one of his top three favorite *SNL* hosts he's interacted with based on her kindness alone.

Now, my friends, comes the time when I tell you how I embarrassed myself in front of one of my heroes.

It was 1989, when Christine Zander, a writer on *SNL*, was back home in Chicago during the show's summer hiatus. Through a few connections, my theater group and I were able to secure a meeting with her and try to convince her to direct our next show, *The Book of Blanche*. If the *Parks* cast's appearance on *Jimmy Fallon* represented the apex of my singing and dancing career, *The Book of Blanche* was its start. A slow start. I don't mean for the show—that became a minor hit, at least in the parlance of musical comedies in Chicago—but for me. Of the six performers, only two could sing . . . and I wasn't one of them.

Christine Zander and I soon became fast friends, and I didn't feel ashamed telling her about my obsession with sitcoms, particularly with Mary Tyler Moore. While Zander could've shrugged off my rantings, instead she recalled our conversations. A few weeks after our show's run, when she was back in NYC, she called to tell me that MTM—yes, I'm allowed to call her that—was going to host *SNL*.

And?!?!

"Well, why don't you guys come out and see the show? You can meet MTM," she said. I'm pretty sure I made some sort of ridiculous screeching noise.

You see, I'd been in Chicago my whole life and never had the opportunity to meet anyone famous. I was raised in Lansing, Illinois, by a pipe-coverer father and a mostly stay-at-home mother. People like us didn't become "famous." That said, I was obsessed with CBS Saturday night television, where comedy could bring together my parents and my siblings, all of whom were different, around a postage-stamp TV. Stars like Mary Tyler Moore, Dick Van Dyke, Carroll O'Connor, and Carol Burnett all had a tremendous influence on my career because they were the ones on TV, week to week, in millions of households. If they could unite my family, couldn't they unite many others? Couldn't they change the world?

But a trip to New York to meet one of my heroes wouldn't have been in my budget. Few things were at the time except for the one pot I had to piss in. However, a couple of us from our theater crowd scraped together enough money to fly out and procure a hotel room. There were five of us in one tiny Manhattan hotel room, but I didn't care. I was going to the Big Apple for the one and only Mary Tyler Moore. The others? For Elvis Costello, that week's musical guest.

I've seen up close and personal how demanding and hard the *SNL* schedule is. It's a bullet train that begins on Monday and pulls into the station the following Saturday night. Scripts are written, rehearsed, edited, and often scrapped at the very last minute. I know it drives people crazy when they notice the performers reading cue cards, but they often don't have a choice. There's every possibility that what they're about to say they're also seeing for the first time. Not just that, but they're live on air. It's so chaotic that there's a hired hand who's responsible for grabbing that week's guest host and moving them from place to place.

Unless you're MTM. We had the great privilege of watching her nail her rehearsals, engaging in off-screen banter and taking notes without breaking a sweat. I was within ten to fifteen feet of her at most times. My pal Zander, sensing my anxiety, asked me: "Want me to introduce you?" If MTM hadn't shown a hint of nervousness during rehearsals, I was like a kid preparing to dive from the high board for the first time. "No," I replied. "I don't think so. Not yet."

I was a total fanboy but too apprehensive to talk to her. I whiffed at the opportunity every time Zander asked me, and I flaked out yet again at the final rehearsal prior to the on-air performance.

I had one chance left. After the Saturday show, Zander invited us to the famous (read: notorious) *SNL* after-party. I won't recount the stories that have been told by the likes of Chevy Chase, Tina Fey, Lorne Michaels, Adam Sandler, and so on, but suffice it to say that the parties were so celebrity jammed that Donald Trump would come all the time, even though nobody invited him or ever wanted him there. Is that a surprise to anyone?

At the after-party, I saw Mary Tyler Moore sitting at a table with her husband, Dr. Robert Levine, and *SNL*'s legendary producer and creator, Lorne Michaels. I kept staring at their table, trying to summon my courage to go and say hello. I couldn't do it no matter how hard I tried to steel myself. Finally, Patrick, one of my buddies in our group, walked up to me and said, "Jim, she's leaving. If you're going to say hello, then this is your last chance." He was right. This was my last chance to talk to my comedy hero and tell her what she meant to me. I hurried over toward the door as she gathered her coat and was able to somehow position my body in front of her.

And then . . .

I froze.

Here I was, this goofy aspiring actor with a broad smile, blocking MTM from her exit. She kept fiddling with her coat to distract herself from the awkwardness ensuing. Her husband, the doctor, remained calm but vigilant. Meanwhile, I remained dumbstruck or struck dumb, I still don't know.

After a beat or two, Mary Tyler Moore sensed something was amiss. She wasn't afraid—I could see that on her face, likely due to the fact that this wasn't a party where just anyone could walk in off the street—but her smile had turned placid, like someone had stuck it on. I could only assume, years after the fact, that the

Mary Tyler Moore, I'm in awe of you!

world-renowned actress jumped to what was perhaps the only logical conclusion: while I smiled and she smiled and I refused to speak, just kept smiling, she assumed that I had an intellectual disability.

It was only after coming to this conclusion—again, a logical one—that her face brightened. Her tone was sweet when she very slowly and deliberately said, "Hi there, I'm Mary. How are you?"

This was the point at which I should've converted my silence to affability, but I said nothing. Stood there and kept smiling. Nodded my head up and down. Slow, then fast, then slow again. The important thing to remember here is that under any normal circumstances I can talk to anyone. As a matter of fact, I'm sure there are many people over the years who have wished I would just STFU. As Ralph Kramden of *The Honeymooners* used to say . . . I'm a BLAAAABBERMOUTH!

"Would you like to take a picture with me?" MTM asked. She knew I wasn't going to break the silence.

I nodded and she copied this gesture, as if I were a baby trying solids for the first time. *Do you like this? Yes, you doooooo. Yes, you do, little Jimmy!*

While I remained frozen, she moved next to me. That's when my friends, cruel savages that they are, snapped a picture. "Well, it was very nice meeting you," she said. I still hadn't said a word. I'm not joking. In a minute's time, I hadn't managed a peep.

She started walking away, and go figure, it occurred to me that I *was* capable of speaking, that I'd been capable the entire time. Did I say anything normal? Of course not. What I managed to get out was this classic admission: "I'm in awe of you!"

She fastened her coat, looked at me a final time, and as sweet as I always knew she would be, replied, "I'm in awe of you, too, Jim!" And then?

Then she was gone.

My buddies had watched this embarrassing scene with bemusement and utter confusion. I'm sure they were thinking what I was moments after MTM walked out of the after-party: *Dude, are you okay? What the heck did you do?* They're still my friends, my regular poker buddies. To this day they taunt me with the occasional "I'm in awe of you." Ahh . . . friends. LOL.

If acting requires looking into the future and forward toward the next gig, the next glint of spotlight, it also involves looking back—stacking our little blunders as lessons for self-improvement. All these years later, I think about what I could've said to MTM. I wonder if anything would've made a difference or impact. Likely not.

You see, Mary Tyler Moore, like Megan, was probably stopped

a hundred times a day, every day, on her way to one errand or another. That's a kind of attention that I don't envy. It takes a lot for someone to be receptive to loads of opinions and questions and maintain composure and peace of mind. The fact she didn't bolt out the door when I went up to her is a testament to her patience.

If fans tell MTM, a comedy queen, stuff along the lines of "I'm in awe of you!," what do you think they say to me?

Well, when the character for which you're best known is described as having "the largest penis that this doctor has ever seen," you can probably anticipate the questions that come my way.

And, yes, guys, it's true . . .

Kidding! (Or am I?) Christie Brinkley is less shallow than that.

Hey, it could be a lot worse—I mean, what if the writers had included a bit about Jerry having the smallest penis a doctor has ever seen? Imagine the questions then. As if Jerry needed more characteristics about which to be teased! For the record, we did shoot an "alt" version of the doctor talking about my visit, in which he says right to the camera, "That man has the smallest penis I have ever seen." I'm eternally grateful they went with the version they did.

I like to think that Jerry Gergich is the Li'l Sebastian of the crew: you may not understand him (especially if you're Ben), but you celebrate him anyway!

An ardent fan would know that Jerry and Li'l Sebastian have more in common than that: They're on the same diabetes medication! They both have huge penises!

At one point in the episode "Harvest Festival," Li'l Sebastian's nether regions are blurred. This was not called for in the script—what I mean is that Tom Haverford wasn't supposed to look at Li'l Sebastian and announce, "Wow, that is a shockingly huge mini horse erection." That li'l guy was hard for hours while shooting; turns out this is a normal biological response and has nothing to do with being "turned on." After trying to wait out the erection, the producers decided that we had to start shooting something. Someone had the wise idea to blur it out in post-production, and a writer decided to give Tom that fantastic line. Perhaps Jerry and Li'l Sebastian's commonalities were best served via Ron Swanson's jocular wisdom: "[Li'l Sebastian] has the legs of Tom, the endurance of Jerry, and the diseases of Jerry." Amen.

Is now a bad time to tell you that Li'l Sebastian dies? In the season finale, yes (episode 16, "Li'l Sebastian"), but in real life, too. Turns out that little guy was pretty old (going on twenty years) when we filmed with him. Two years after *Parks* wrapped, I had a recurring role on a show called *Bless This Mess,* in which all kinds of animals made appearances. One afternoon on set, I spotted the animal trainer who had worked with us on "Harvest Festival," in which Li'l Sebastian appeared several years before. On this set, she was working with a pig and chickens, but I couldn't help remembering her with Li'l Sebastian, feeding him apples and petting him as the rest of us looked on adoringly. I gave the li'l guy plenty of apples myself. It's so funny when you realize that the smile you see on Ron's face when I first bring in Li'l Sebastian during "Harvest Festival" is a genuine reflection of Nick's mood at the time. Such a mensch, that guy.

Oh, right, the animal trainer. So I walked up to her and asked, "How's our li'l friend doing?" She knew immediately whom I was referring to.

"Li'l Sebastian, he's passed," she said. (His real name was Gideon.) I think she noticed that I was getting some wet eyes, so she added, "Don't worry, Jim. He had a good life. A good stage life, too. He was in movies and TV for over twenty years." Was that supposed to make me feel better? It didn't.

I knew that Li'l Sebastian didn't belong to *Parks*—an animal doesn't belong to anyone!—but it felt like he had signed up for our wild and crazy family. And how much we loved him! I bet if the shirt you see Ben wearing at the end of "Harvest Festival" hadn't been created for the episode, the crew would've made it anyway.

To this day, I haven't told the rest of the *Parks* cast what I was told that day on *Bless This Mess*. It's as if I've been trying to preserve his image in our collective heart. Maybe I've been doing something else, too: by not discussing it with my castmates, I've

I love this li'l horse so much. RIP, Li'l Sebastian.

delayed our collective sadness. I'm sure they know by now that Li'l Sebastian is no longer with us—they don't live under rocks—but if not, and if they're just finding out now, forgive me for not saying anything. (The spirit of Li'l Sebastian lives on.)

"Harvest Festival" is a good example of *Parks'* bleeding heart. There's the happy ending in the form of the crew pulling off a successful event, despite Joan Callamezzo's attempts to thwart it; there's Ron yelling at the top of the Ferris wheel for everyone to apologize to one another (which Jerry desperately needs because Tom is being such a dick!); and, of course, there's Li'l Sebastian himself, being all cute and old and a perfect encapsulation of the kind of thing that Pawnee citizens love but cannot explain. This episode helped clarify why I loved *Parks* in the first place, why I always will: because as much as it is a comedy set within an office, it is also a glimpse into a subculture of community, sometimes tethered together and sometimes bursting at the seams (and sometimes peppered with some Native American curses against those dreadful barbarous white folk).

"Harvest Festival" also, quite literally, took a community to make happen. The producers rented a huge empty lot in Woodland Hills, California, that was adjacent to a cornfield and used every hand we had to build the set from scratch. Not only that, but they brought in tents, rides, food vendors, and a crapload of extras to walk around. The only thing that was not fabricated was the roller coaster you see at the end of the episode, which was CGI. Other than that, what you see was built and enjoyed specifically by us and for us. Even the Ferris wheel scene, made possible by a crane shot. I discovered while filming this scene that Nick gets motion sickness, but in typical Nick fashion he never mentioned it and plowed through like the trooper he is.

Shooting the Ferris wheel scene was one of those moments where, suspended a couple hundred feet in the air and howling out to Nick between takes, I thought about how lucky I was to be part of such a special group.

In my teenage years, I craved a sense of community so badly, even if I wasn't prepared to join one. Because back then, in my hometown of Chicago, the theater community I aspired to join was looked down upon. In my high school—though I'm sure this is a cliché all the world over—four categories reigned supreme: you had your jocks, "regular kids," burnouts, and—sad and pathetic, this label, though not my creation—"theater fags." I cringe even writing that word. As a "regular kid," and someone who, I believed, got along with everyone, I dreamed about the shared passions that united the theater kids. They were also original, in their creativity and style. They marched to the beat of their own drummer, and, best of all, they were onstage! Maybe the jocks had their own stage, in the form of a soccer field or baseball diamond, but nobody was waiting for them to slip up on a line or botch a high note. In fact, they were praised even when they were making mistakes—how coddled jocks can be! But the theater kids? They had to deal with adversity in the form of name-calling and *still* get onstage, night after night, performance after performance, and act to the best of their abilities.

I feared that spotlight and the negative attention I thought it fostered. I feared failing.

While the theater kids got to pretend to be in the South Pacific or in the dust bowl of Oklahoma, I pretended . . . in the confines of my bedroom. I was John Travolta holding a guitar and belting out "Greased Lightnin'." Or the Cowardly Lion wishing he only had a brain . . . I mean a heart . . . the nerve. But in the hallways of school? I considered myself too cool to join those curtain climbers on one adventure or the next. All of this fear, anxiety, and jealousy compounded during my senior year when I watched Charles B. Edelstein, the resident theater geek with the best voice I'd ever heard back then, belt out a song from *South Pacific*: "Some enchanted evening, / When you find your true love . . ." The applause for Charles was electric, and the reception after contagious. And for good reason: legend Andrew Lloyd Webber once called this the greatest song ever written for a musical. Nobody ever said that about Joey the Jock scoring his fifth goal of the soccer season. At that moment, I wanted to be Charles. I wanted the fearlessness and bravery I watched in his performance.

I've already told you that it took me years to wear that cape of bravery, and it was well past my stint at Loyola University and Midwestern Broadcasting School that I even considered acting as a career, never mind a hobby. But *South Pacific* opened an avenue for me that day, even if it wasn't fully drivable just yet. It showed me that public performance didn't have to be as scary (or as geeky) as I might have thought.

That year, I became president of DECA (Distributive Education Clubs of America), which encourages business and marketing skills through academic conferences and competitions. In retrospect, that's probably even nerdier than getting up onstage and singing your heart out, but what did I know at the time? Ignorance aside, DECA propelled my secret love for public speaking, which I had craved through the likes of Charles and the brave nerdy kids who performed with him and all the musicals I was watching at home. As president, I was tasked with organizing fundraisers and parties, whereby I also bestowed upon myself the role of master of ceremonies. While I could have shared some of that "stage time," I enjoyed giving speeches and pumping up my peers. Those scenes in *The Wolf of Wall Street* where Leo DiCaprio riles up his ethically deranged colleagues and receives a standing ovation? That was based on me, not Jordan Belfort. Who the heck is Jordan Belfort anyway?*

Yikes! Who the hell found this picture?

I was able to inherit that sense of community—you're reading a book by a cast member of one of the greatest ensemble shows ever created. But if my problem at high school had been relating to peers my age, how did I fare connecting with people much younger than me, on a prime-time set, no less?

The difference between me and Aziz was stark. For one thing, he was obsessed with his phone while I'd just learned how to connect to a hotspot. Part of this was due to his age—being twenty-something and wading through the dizzying freedom of possibility. The other part of it was that, quite simply, Aziz was *not* like the rest of us. Like I said, he wasn't a trained actor. He was a rising star in the comedy world who had been plucked out of it and asked to give acting a shot. And he didn't need to! He

---

* Let me have this. My delusion helps me sleep at night.

didn't need acting nor a show like *Parks* to prove his clout; he already had it. Meanwhile, I needed *Parks*. I'd been blessed to have a busy career pre-*Parks*, but it's no secret that getting cast in *Parks* changed my life.

I don't know if Aziz's phone use was due to his being a millennial, but dude was on his phone a lot. And before you come down on me for technology-shaming, understand that my opinions are not born from jealousy or from world-weariness. I simply want to know what Aziz was watching on his phone that was so freaking exciting! I'm reminded of season 5's "Sex Education," in which Tom is banned from using devices for a week after getting into a car accident, caused by his addiction to his screen. In the episode, Tom's device is taken away mid-text, and Tom hilariously screams, "Press send, Bailiff. Press send!"

At some point, I think during the third season, a memo from producers circulated that said phones were henceforth banned on set. Naturally, we called this the Aziz Memo. While we all knew the memo was about him, it affected all of us because now we couldn't be on our phones either, at least not as obviously.

Aziz's phone obsession could be a bit distracting. Sometimes between takes, actors like to run lines with one another to get them down pat, and many times Aziz wouldn't make himself available to do that. This didn't make the relationship between Aziz and the rest of the cast feel tenuous, not at all, but it simply meant he and I came from separate worlds. His was one of comedy tours and parties with Jay-Z and Beyoncé and Snake Juice at the Snakehole Lounge (if such a thing existed off-screen), and mine consisted of brunch with my lovable aunts and taking my dogs to the vet for annual shots. Both couldn't have been more different, but neither style is right or wrong.

He was young, though, and likely obsessed with social media. I think he was taking the work seriously, with his stand-up shows and a variety of other projects, but there was only so much time in a day. But every actor has their own process, and he brought good stuff to every scene he was in.

Something changed in our dynamic when he invited me to the Orpheum in Los Angeles in 2012 to see one of his stand-up specials. I brought a friend, someone younger and hipper than I who could translate Aziz's jokes to me because . . . well . . . I didn't understand them either. Chelsea Peretti,* who starred in another Mike Schur production, *Brooklyn Nine-Nine*, was his opener and just killed it. I was laughing my ass off. After Chelsea took her bows, it was time for Aziz to hit the stage. This young kid whom I'd been working with had filled this huge auditorium, and the fresh-faced people around me were screaming for him. (I got the occasional "Damn it, Jerry" thrown my direction.)

While the audience began losing their minds, it dawned on me that I was not Aziz's target market. I didn't understand a lot of the jokes. They involved people and places and objects I'd never heard of. Want to know how I knew this? In front of me, behind me, to my left, and to my right were kids. No, not kids-kids, but younger people. People with flashy cell phones and snazzy hats and shoes and who made references to "handles" and "followers." I had love handles.

I kid you not, the crowd went crazy. *Delirium*–era–Eddie Murphy crazy. Or as close to it as I've ever seen in real life. Everything Aziz said, which to me sounded like an inside joke I was eavesdropping on, was met by rapturous laughter and applause.

---

* Who also wrote two episodes of *Parks*, in case you didn't know.

After the show, my friend and I went backstage to meet Aziz and talk to him over some drinks and snacks. "How did you enjoy the show?" Aziz asked us.

"Aziz," I said, harrumphing, "I didn't understand a fucking word you were talking about." He laughed. "But everyone else?" I continued. "They freaking loved it!" I patted him on the back and told him what a good job he'd done and how I admired his stage presence. Just because I didn't get the references doesn't mean the jokes weren't any good. They were, clearly! I also got to tell Chelsea that she was amazing up there.

The series "wrap day" with Aziz. No, not "rap day."

My relationship with Aziz changed after his performance at the Orpheum. While it was apparent we were never going to run a TikTok channel together (or in those days a Facebook page), we could be sure that we supported each other onstage and off-. I realized Aziz was driven by the same compulsion as the rest of us actors, that strong undercurrent of needing recognition. In the same way that Charles from high school wasn't just performing to an audience of one during our senior year, we weren't acting to curry favor from only ourselves. We were acting to get a laugh, a cry, an enthusiastic shout. We were acting and then asking, like Aziz had, "How did you enjoy the show?" And then secretly hoping that they'd say they loved it and return.

Where Are My Guardians?

As my fellow friends and castmates were achieving big things on the show and beyond, I was feeling less enthusiastic about my own professional progress. Nick had procured a book deal, Aziz's stand-up career was soaring, Pratt had been cast in a little movie called *Zero Dark Thirty*, and Adam Scott was being hired for a ton of projects (five films between 2011 and 2012 alone). The ladies of *Parks* were also killing it outside the show. Meanwhile, I had been getting my slow trickle of TV and film opportunities, but most were smaller fare, not the career-altering kind I was hoping for.

By season 4, Jerry had become a lovable lug to fans, but I was always secretly afraid Jerry would go bye-bye, either immediately dissolved or dwindled down in the service of other regular series members' roles. That's why I was so keen on receiving opportunities outside of *Parks*—because if Jerry were banished, then at least he'd have a proper "Elba" to go to.

I didn't know *Parks* would last another season, let alone three. Other than the last two seasons, there was always a fear of cancellation, and each season we'd have to wait until the upfronts from the network in May to know if we were coming back for another season or not. We'd text with Mike Schur or Amy to see if they'd heard anything, and when they said they hadn't, we'd sometimes scan the internet for comments and articles about us. If the media was talking, we thought we were safe. If they weren't, we thought we were gone. Sometimes it was the reverse—talk about a mind-fuck! But getting the news of the pickup was always such a high. It meant more work for me and another year with that amazing cast and crew.

But when a cast and crew are as close as we were, each person's success reminds you of your failures.

I had to speak with my agents at the time to discover why

I wasn't getting many auditions, and I solicited my manager Lynda's help. In so many words, I told the agents I was disappointed I wasn't getting more prominent bookings. Forget bookings, I said, how about auditions? It was nerve-racking, but this was my career.

"We're doing everything we can," my agents told me.

"Well, I'm not seeing that," I said.

"Look," they said, "we'll show you. Starting now, we'll provide documentation to you of all the places we're submitting you to. So you can see that it's the industry as a whole. We're trying."

Lynda, not wanting to rock the boat, told me we should give them another chance. I agreed—as much as I like Jimmy Buffett, I'm no boat-rocker either.

Weeks passed and there was still no documentation from the agents that showed what they were submitting me for. It's hard enough to be turned down for roles and to ask why, but to see no proof that you're even being submitted or in the mix? That's humiliating. I realized I had to change something, and I needed advice from someone outside the immediate situation. From someone whose career choices I had always admired.

In between scenes one day, I walked up to Amy. "Do you mind if I get your opinion on something?" I asked her. I told her about the situation, about how neither Lynda nor I wanted to make my agents upset. How I didn't know if my agents at the time were working for me or against me, or whether I was simply overthinking all of this, which I tend to do sometimes. "What do I do?" I begged. "I really feel like I have no option but to fire them. Am I wrong?"

Amy half smiled and said to me, "Look, you have to remember," she said, "that these agents have hundreds of clients. You only have you. You can't worry about how they're going to feel. They have two hundred, three hundred, four hundred actors who are helping to pay their bills. Your money is made by the work that *you* and only you do." In an instant, Amy had changed my perspective on an issue that had been bugging me for months. I could've hugged her right then and there.

This wasn't the first or last time Amy had provided career advice. When we filmed season 3, episode 16, "Li'l Sebastian," I had received an actual offer from my agents (the same ones mentioned above) to play a character who's a pedophile. There are no degrees of vileness for a pedophile, but if there were, this character would've been among the vilest. The script characterized him as wealthy and someone who enjoyed flying around the world to meet kids in specialized quarters; at one point, after a young female character around nine years old is brought in to meet him and then departs the scene, the pedophile reprimands his assistant: "I told you I wanted young!" That's the kind of vile I'm referring to. I thought about taking on this role as a type of acting challenge, the kind I'd dreamed about all those years before when taking classes at Second City. But I had serious reservations. Amy, after hearing my gross-out of a recap, wisely said, "Jim, you're going to be a big comedy guy after *Parks*. This show is going to change everything." She was right of course. Whether it was comedy or drama I'd pursue, *Parks* was going to open doors previously closed to me. So, it wasn't a question that I'd listen to Amy this time around either. Some roles you don't want to be known for, and a sick pedophile is pretty much near the top of that list. Amy's assessment and judgment of this opportunity should have been shared by my agents.

Suffice it to say that once you make it known to agents that you're unhappy, word gets out quickly. In turn, they were likely less willing to work on behalf of someone they knew would leave, but nothing in my contract prevented me from talking to other professionals. I was gathering information, one potential agent at a time.

I eventually signed on with Stone Manners, who within two weeks of collecting my ink brought me a terrific gig on a movie. I was blown away. I had been so worried I was the problem and that nobody wanted to cast me, but this was proof that it wasn't just my sensitivity—the jobs were out there, and they could be mine. Beyond the gigs that started to roll in, there were so many other things Stone Manners did to made me feel supported: they took me out to dinner, they sent me birthday cards, they even bought me gifts like iPods each time a new season commenced (a show they weren't earning a commission on initially). In our seventeen years together, my former agents had taken me to dinner once; I had them over to my house for dinner twice. Never did they call to wish me luck on the new season. (Although I did get birthday cards, which I always appreciated.) In their defense, I've come to believe they just didn't know better—they only had so much clout to make certain calls and perhaps didn't realize what other agents were doing for their clients on series. Or perhaps they were treating other clients different from me for a reason I will never understand. Ultimately, every actor thinks they're not getting enough attention, that they're not being submitted for everything they think they're right for. Though the turmoil caused by my switching agencies created some grief for Lynda, she agreed it was the best move for my career. Both of us have never looked back.

The plan has always been this: stay busy, stay inspired, and stay happy. Unfortunately, two major things happened during season 4 that stained my happy-go-lucky view. The first was *People* magazine's shoot for "The Men of *Parks and Recreation*," where it was decided that any person identifying as a male character on the show would be invited to take part in a photo shoot that would grace the pages of the glossy mag. In 2011, this was a big deal. Not only was *Parks* the hit show on TV, but *People* was one of the biggest celebrity magazines on newsstands. In my opinion, *People* has always been one of the most reliable entertainment news sources. To be included in a feature like that might have provided a nice career boost, not to mention an appreciation of my role on the show.

And the feature turned out beautiful! Black-and-white photos of "the guys" in expensive tuxes as they're punching and regaling one another with jokes, like bachelors at some elite wedding. There are even cabaret dancers with feather boas silhouetted in the back of some shots.

The only thing missing? Me.

Okay . . . and Rob Lowe, but it's only because Rob had a scheduling conflict.

People hadn't even asked me! I only found out because the shoot happened on a soundstage steps from my trailer. I was heading back to take a load off when I heard cabaret music and my castmates' laughter and jokes. Camera flashes lit up the place. I was curious, sure, but thought nothing of it—photo shoots for behind-the-scenes material happen all the time on a soundstage. I asked a production assistant what was happening and they explained that my fellow bros were dressed up for a magazine feature on the men of *Parks*.

The cabaret music and laughter felt like it'd turned into a

minor-key melody of mockery. I wanted to run from it, bury myself inside my trailer, and not reappear until the shoot was over. For the first time in several years, I'd been made to feel like the insecure journeyman actor that had been cast in this show—not so much part of the family as adjacent to it, a substitute rather than a starter. Luckily, I had my ride-or-die next to me again.

Retta listened as I poured my heart out. "If they were doing a 'Ladies of *Parks*,'" I remember her saying, "then I would feel the same. That really sucks." I thought how that wouldn't be the same, that my pal Retta doesn't suffer fools and would've given *People* a piece of her mind (which she never had to do because they would include her in a "Ladies of *Parks*" piece, and rightfully so).

Chris Pratt and Me

ME: I remember you, particularly more than some others, being worried about some of the Jerry bits being . . . mean. I remember you saying, "Jimmy, you okay with these?" My theory was, "It's funny and these are just jobs. I'm happy to be around." Do you remember that feeling at all?

CHRIS: I do, I do. I was concerned in some of those moments because I care about you and I love you, and I knew that there were some jokes that were, like, mean. But meaner than they were funny. If it's a joke, it's funny. But if it's mean for the sake of being mean, well, I'm not a huge fan of mean-spirited humor, and I just wanted to check in on you. There was one time where I put my foot down on something. [*Jim laughs*] There was that time you use the printer and it says something like "Jerry sucks" on a piece of paper, and I just said, "I don't think that's funny. I don't know about it." For the most part, I rolled with it, but there were a couple times where I think it went too far and I was concerned for you.

ME: We're human beings, yeah. And just so you know, that meant the world to me. You checked in on me, Amy checked in on me, and it's not like I expected everyone to check in on me, but the fact that you did was so special.

CHRIS: Well, I also know that we're from the Midwest, and people from the Midwest—their love language is, like, teasing. You learn to take your lumps and roll with it—I did at least—and I was never overly concerned you couldn't take care of yourself, but if it ever went too far, I wanted you to know I was there for you.

ME: You have the biggest heart, and I don't mean it from a medical perspective. But you haven't changed who you are, you haven't changed your values, you're still the nicest man I met on *Parks*. Especially in this online world—I can't imagine the crap that is said online.

CHRIS: I've partly grown accustomed to it. It's part of what the world is. My world and *the world*. It's a strange thing. In the past ten years the way social media has changed the story we believe about ourselves is crazy. I thank God I have the faith in me and the faith that I was raised with, because it's a real whirlwind if you don't have a strong foundation on the ground. And you know what happens? The world eats it up. They love it.

ME: They love to build you up and they love to take you down, dude. That's how it works.

CHRIS: Entertainment value. To worship an idol and then to burn an idol.

They say that luck—both good and bad—comes in threes, and this was true come season 4. First the matter of switching agents, then the *People* shoot, and finally, most heartbreaking, the death of my mother. All of that in the span of a few months. What people say about losing a parent is true, too: It doesn't matter how old you are or whether you expected it. A loss of this caliber stings for a long, long time. And since I'm a mama's boy through and through, this loss hit hard.

That's not to say I didn't love my father—of course I did—but he never truly understood the acting business. He was raised with seven other brothers and sisters by a cop and a teacher. When it came time to raise his own family, my dad's priority in life was giving his wife and children a good, safe home. So much so that he gave up what he enjoyed most to make more money for them. Originally a sheriff's officer, he turned to the trades when he realized the salary was a heck of a lot higher, becoming an insulator for Krez before working for M&O Insulation (a company his brother cofounded). He died in 1991 after a four-month battle with lung cancer, way before he could see my career take off.

I'm grateful that my mom got to see some of my success before she passed. After moving to Los Angeles in 1994, I'd been on many different TV shows (and some films) over the years, and Mom would love telling her friends and family what I was doing. She was always my first call whether I had good news following an audition or bad. A mama's boy, I said? Oh, you betcha.

Mom had the opportunity to visit me many times over the years. One time she came to Vancouver while I was filming a remake of *Harvey* with Leslie Nielsen, Swoosie Kurtz, Harry Anderson, and Jonathan Banks, among others. The producers sent a car to take her from the airport to set because I was filming by the time she'd arrived. The scene took place outside of a bar and I had to run into a phone booth to make a call. For the

shot, they'd shut down the street and lit up the sky with moon lights. It was quite the production. When I finished my take and saw my mom, I ran over to say hi and realized she was crying. I asked her what was wrong, and she said, "This is all for you?" I explained that it was for a scene in the film, but in her mind this was all for her "little Jimmy." I think that was the first time it occurred to her that it might all work out for me.

When I landed the role of Jerry, I called her immediately. "This is it," she rejoiced. "I think this is the one. The big one." Typically neurotic, I immediately shut her down and told her that it probably wouldn't go more than a season. Thankfully my mom was right. She always was. My success, in return, made it feel like I didn't let down her and Dad.

A year and a half prior to when we started filming season 4, my mom was diagnosed with lung cancer. Devastated though

Me and Swoosie Kurtz shooting a remake of <u>Harvey</u> in Vancouver—one of my first lead roles. Incredibly exciting.

we were, my siblings (Beth, John, and Ann) and I put on brave faces and told her that we'd be with her every step of the way. Oncology visits, radiation, spa days, whatever she needed. My siblings and I understood the importance our presence held. After all, we had lost our father to lung cancer, when he was only fifty-seven. Our dad's timeline from diagnosis to death was a mere four months, so it was essential that none of us overlooked or overestimated our time with Mom. That's who we were, how we were brought up—with the knowledge that nothing in this life is guaranteed except the time we have with one another.

In fact, we might be too close. Allow me, please, a quick digression before we get back to Mom: When my dad was sick, he was being treated at Rush-Presbyterian hospital in Chicago, an amazing facility and well-known as a teaching hospital. While there, one of the young residents asked some routine questions prior to trying some last-minute radiation to help my father regain his speech. "Has the patient had any prior surgeries?" the resident asked. I'm quite certain the doc was asking about a history of surgeries that would affect any outcomes before trying the next round of treatment, but my mother, speaking for my father, blurted out, "Well, here goes the family secret!" My siblings and I looked at one another with a *WTF is she about to say* look on our faces. And then she did, she said it: "Twenty-five years ago, he had a vasectomy, Doctor." *A VASECTOMY? Our Irish Catholic father had opted for permanent birth control? Are you kidding me?* My dad and one of his best friends had gone to get vasectomies, like one gets group tattoos. Mom told us in the days after the reveal at the doctor's office, trying to defend Dad's decision, "Every time your father looked at me, I got pregnant." If we weren't scarred before then, we were now. That slight trauma brought us a little closer.

Initially, my mom questioned whether she even wanted to fight her cancer. She had seen many friends and loved ones lose that battle. After lots of begging and pleading, we convinced her that it was worth the fight to be here for her kids and grandkids. And by the time we'd begun shooting season 4, life was as good as it could've been given the circumstances: Mom's cancer was in remission, her energy was back, and her spirits were high. This healthy period also witnessed her vanity in top form. One day, she accompanied me into town to food-shop but told me she wouldn't be getting out of the car. "I don't want the neighbors to see me with a walker," she said.

"Mom, who cares about that?"

"I do, Jimmy!"

Fair enough. Another thing we'd learned over seventy-odd years of her raising me and my siblings: there's no arguing with that woman.

Those few months of perceived health were a blessing, but as season 4's filming continued, Mom's condition started to worsen. Scans revealed that the cancer was back. This time, the prognosis was dire and Mom refused to go back into treatment. We couldn't blame her and quickly fell in line with whatever she wanted. We didn't want to argue this time either; we didn't want to make her feel worse.

She was treated palliatively, and we did everything in our power to help mitigate her pain. But when the doctors suggested that she undergo a tracheotomy to help her breathe better and give her maybe a few more weeks of life, Mom told us she'd had enough. Who could blame her? We tried, gently and tactfully, to convince her, but we didn't want to add undue pressure.

We hired a woman named Nina, a home health care worker from Poland, to help with late-stage care. She spoke broken English and could be very direct at times, but she took incredible care of our mother. The Monday before my mom passed away, things looked grim. My siblings and I were gathered around the hospital bed that we had set up in her living room, praying and watching her every breath. My nieces asked for alone time with "Gram" to talk with her and say their goodbyes. Nina asked me what was going on, and when I explained that we were sure that this was the end, that Mom would leave us any minute, Nina corrected me: "No. Mommy not go tonight." I didn't know what to say to her, but I was sure she was wrong.

Well, it appeared Nina was correct, because the next morning my mother was sitting up in bed, alert and eating a Popsicle. She seemed to have more energy than we'd seen in weeks. I couldn't believe it. I was thrilled that my mom seemed better and shocked that Nina had some insight that the rest of us didn't.

At around 10 p.m. the following Friday night, I noticed that Nina was cooking something in the kitchen, which seemed odd because she would normally go to bed around 9 p.m. and get up periodically to check on my mom. I asked Nina what she was doing up so late, and she said, "Mommy go tonight." *What? No. She's still hydrated, and her breathing seems stable. How can that be?* Nina walked me over to my mom and showed me the signs that she knew all too well. The mottling of the skin. The shallow breaths. The punctuated moments of silence. One minute I'm praying for my mom to pass away peacefully to end her suffering and then, when it's actually happening, I'm asking God to let her live. Even though there had been time to say what needed to be said, I wasn't ready to say goodbye. But Nina was right. At 1:16 a.m. on December 31, 2011, Eileen O'Keefe O'Heir died. As did a part of me.

As I've said, there's never a good time for anyone to die, let alone your own mother, but I was grateful to spend a couple solid weeks with her and not have to worry about work as we were on holiday hiatus.

My mom did everything to make it easier on us when she knew her time was limited. She had written letters to us. She had told us where to find all her documents that we would need for matters of the estate. She also . . . totally screwed me over! Yes, this sweet, wonderful woman whom I've been telling you about stuck it to me in the end. Okay, that sounds terrible, so let me explain: After my mom passed and we were making funeral arrangements, I told my siblings there was no way I would be able to speak at Mom's funeral. I knew I'd be a bucket of tears and wouldn't be able to get through it. I also knew my siblings would expect me to speak because I'm the guy who's been in front of people and cameras for years. But my siblings understood and agreed that I didn't have to speak if I didn't feel comfortable doing so. One day, as we were at my mom's house and going through the papers she'd left for us, I spotted an envelope on a paper stack with these words written on it: *Jimmy. Please read this at my funeral.* Seriously? I'd just convinced my brother and sisters I wasn't going to get up and talk at the funeral, but here was a directive from beyond the grave. Of course, I had no choice but to follow through on her wishes.

I went over it and over it, each time crying my eyes out. I thought if I cried enough beforehand I'd be mostly composed when the time came to read it at the funeral mass. But guess what? It doesn't work that way. I cried like a little baby while trying to get out the words my mom had written. Between the sobs and gasps, I'm not sure if anybody heard anything I said. It doesn't matter,

The O'Heirs, a perfect encapsulation of our happy family.

though: I was able to carry out one last request for Mom.

I still talk to my parents in my head. I believe that when I pass, they'll both be there waiting for me. As much as I'm not looking for that to happen any time soon, I will not be afraid when it's my time. Mom and Dad will be there to show me the ropes.

Between my mother's diagnosis and making the arrangements after she passed, the production team at *Parks* was more than accommodating of my occasional need to reschedule and take some time away from set. There are shows that wouldn't give a rat's ass whether it's someone's birthday or funeral; money is money, those producers seem to believe, and you're wasting it. But at *Parks*, the atmosphere that Amy, Greg, and Mike had fostered and grown from day one was different. When I did fly back to Los Angeles to rejoin the cast after Christmas break, I was lucky to meet the loving eyes, ears, and arms of the cast. Naturally, Retta was my emotional sweat towel, suitcase, and sofa rolled into one. I also learned that Retta's an empath. "You cry, I'm gonna cry, too," Retta told me in her trailer, and so it went—me crying and Retta following suit, and a bevy of sweet emotions between us.

You want to cry, too? Hell, I just did remembering this story. We were shooting the episode "Sweet Sixteen," before Christmas break, shortly before my mom passed. There's a scene where Leslie cozies up to Jerry and falls asleep on his shoulder. If you don't recall, this Jerry-centric episode concerns a birthday party that Leslie decides to throw for him. (Because his birthday falls on a leap day, the staff decides that it's his sixteenth birthday instead of his sixty-fourth, a bit that's still so funny—I was forty-nine at the time.) Anyhoo, this being one of those tender scenes—not very different from the one I did with Spader on *Boston Legal*—it required multiple takes. With multiple takes came, of course, time. Lots of it. And time proved to be both a blessing and curse as it pertained to talking about my mother. If I had my preference, I would've chosen nonstop action, dialogue, and movement—things that would've distracted from my sadness and caused me to focus in on the disparate parts of filming a show. I knew that the next day I'd be flying home to Chicago to say goodbye to my mom. I wanted distractions. On the other hand, a scene like this gave me time to slow down and address my thoughts and emotions in the moment. Although when you're performing a scene in which a fellow actor is sleeping on your shoulder, you're not processing these emotions by yourself.

As with the rest of the cast and crew, Amy knew about my mother's illness and always checked in with me about how she was doing. Until now, we hadn't had a moment to talk in detail. Not that I expected it. On the contrary, I was regularly trying to avoid that topic with everyone. But on that day, as Amy laid her head on my shoulder, she and I waxed poetic about all things life and death. We traded personal stories while reminding each other that even though a life ends, the story of a life doesn't have to. It was a lot like being on a show actually. As Amy talked and comforted me, blubbery puddles started deep within my chest and then pooled in my eyes. I swiped away my tears so nobody, especially her, would notice. I was trying my hardest not to cry and appear vulnerable in front of Amy and the crew. I couldn't reply to the sweet things Amy was saying because I was seconds away from losing it.

I've always worried that Amy didn't understand why I was being so quiet. Or if she thought her kind words were falling on deaf ears. It would break my heart if that's what she thought. The truth is that I knew if the floodgates opened, I wasn't going to be able to close them. Who was I kidding? I was Jerry. If anyone was going to appear vulnerable, it was the guy playing him.

Minutes passed, cameras changed positions, key grips gathered new equipment, and still I managed not to cry. To this day, I'm not even sure how I did so. In addition to Retta and Pratt, Amy was one of the people I trusted most on set, and her touching words about family and memory moved me beyond words.

I am struck by one thing above all else—that as I sat there with Amy and tried to prevent the blubbery emotional blob from surfacing, I never thanked her for her kindness and comfort. So, let this printed book be proof, dear Amy, that I've never forgotten the empathy you showed me that day.

Amy, Greg, and Mike had implemented a set brimming with compassion and understanding. And they proved their sympathy through action. Shortly after Mom died, I got a call from Morgan Sackett's secretary. "Hi, Jim," she said, "Morgan and I would like you to know how sorry we are for your loss. We'd like to pay for the catering for after the funeral if that's all right with you."

"What about the funeral itself?" I asked.

Kidding. I *did not* say that! I was too overcome with gratitude to say anything.

I eventually coughed up, "That's so, so nice of you guys, but it's already taken care of. But thank you, this means the world." When one of the camera crew lost her brother around the same time, Morgan extended the same generosity. Maybe he had purchased a group package for funeral catering events.

Amy was our rock. Determined and loyal— she always had our backs.

Kidding again. The guy is a freaking saint.

I often think about "Sweet Sixteen" in the context of my journey at *Parks* and how, like many episodes that came before, it was a turning point in my career. It occurs just after the midpoint of the "middle season" of *Parks*. It's specific to Jerry's story arc, reminding me I had a safe place within the show's ecosystem. It signaled that despite all the adversity I'd faced that year—switching agents, being left out of the *People* photo shoot, and losing my mother to cancer—I was in Los Angeles doing what I loved, involved in a career that my mother had always supported. She wouldn't be able to see that season or the series conclude, but I could sleep peacefully knowing I'd made her proud. And that, for any kid of Midwestern stock and breeding, will always be enough.

Always a Funnier Bit

The bond we shared through season 4 and beyond wasn't limited to us actors either. You could find it just as easily in the writers' room, and the connection we'd made with those brainiacs was integral to the show's success.

"If you were a writer, you wanted to be near the soundstage. And if you were an actor, you wanted to be near the writers," Mike Scully, one of *Parks*' incredible writers, told me in early 2023 when he joined me on a podcast that I cohost (*Parks and Recollection*) about . . . you guessed it. Scully is a force in the comedy-writing world. A onetime executive producer and showrunner for *The Simpsons*, he has worked on numerous celebrated shows and has even won some Emmys along the way. (And get this: Scully hails from Springfield, Massachusetts—yes, the same name as the town in *The Simpsons*. If there's a better coincidence, I can't think of it.) Scully was referring to the writers' habit of "sneaking" onto the soundstage to observe our antics, and, similarly, our habit of wanting to get as close to the writers as possible. "I've been on shows where you had to be careful of what you threw the actors in terms of material," Scully went on to tell me. "But we threw it all at you guys and you'd make magic out of it. It wasn't like that on any other shows I've worked."

That was the creative bond between writers and actors—writers would visit the soundstage to see how their absurd ideas were panning out, and actors would venture upstairs to pitch the writers concepts based on how they experienced their own characters. When I asked Scully if he found this tactic that actors used annoying, he said, "Of course not!" If it was, he's too nice a guy to tell me the truth. Plus, he's a writer. They never tell the truth.

Since the very beginning, our fondness for our characters extended off-screen. I can recall many conversations Pratt and I had about the arc of our characters and how we'd play into them. This is why Andy develops a more sophisticated, self-aware (though no less lovable) personality after season 3, in the same way that Leslie becomes less of an archetype after season 1. Actors see themselves in their characters and play into their invented hopes and dreams. Similarly, the writers had hopes and dreams of their own, which is why the conversations between us and them were so crucial. It wasn't "just another job" for any of us.

Chris Pratt

I was pretty much hired to be a comedic jazz soloist. I loved Andy. I loved playing him. It was probably the easiest job I've ever had. I lived twenty minutes from set, hair and makeup took twenty minutes, I never had to carry any emotional weight. I didn't have a care in life. My winning formula to get out of things in life was to make people laugh. It was like I'd been playing Andy my whole life. People would be like, "You are Andy." And I'd say, "Well no, I'm not ... but actually I am."

One example of the idiosyncrasies that writers and actors bring to the screen occurs in season 4, episode 11, "The Comeback Kid." Early in the episode, Leslie meets with the parks office to appoint her campaign manager for her city council run. Every single character puts their head down in silent but obvious denial—nobody wants that job. Everyone, that is, except for Jerry, who appears optimistic, even determined, to be chosen. But Jerry

Me and Pratt goofing off on set. What a surprise.

Retta never takes a bad photo. (She insists on it!)

wants the task as much as Leslie doesn't want him for it, and, naturally, he's passed up. When I talked to the episode's writer Mike Scully about this choice, I was surprised to learn that he didn't recall Jerry's zeal. He thought Jerry had been just as resistant as the other folks. "Even Jerry doesn't want the job!" Scully said.

"No, no," I replied. "Rewatch the episode. Jerry wants it!" I know that Jerry would never discourage Leslie. I know that he'd always have her back. I know Jerry as well as I know myself.

We laughed about our differing viewpoints—who was right? Mike? Me? Or was it like what Nietzsche said about rightness, something like, "You have your way. I have my way. As for the right way, the correct way, and the only way, it does not exist." (Full disclosure: I found that quote somewhere on the internet. I thought Nietzsche was a type of strudel.) For the record, I told Mike Scully that if the director (Tucker Gates) had suggested I play the scene like Scully had written it, I would've disputed that choice. Call me stubborn, but if I feel committed to a tonal or stylistic choice for a character, I'm going to do it my way. That's the elastic transformation from writing to acting to capturing it on camera—the writers gave us room to roam and we, in turn, were thankful for their trust.

The writing room, from which so many of these brilliant ideas came, was actually a giant wing on the third floor of the Radford lot—we occupied stages 21 and 22—where communal tables and couches were densely packed. Everything from DVDs to reference books to comics to records to scratch pads littered the area. And in one of the big conference rooms stood the most perfect symbol of organized chaos I've ever laid eyes on—an evolving storyboard of the current season, complete with cross-outs, Post-its, and character diagrams that would put CIA headquarters to shame. As the writer Greg Levine told me recently, "Just 'cause something is funny, it still has to be true to a storyline," and nothing expresses this sentiment as much as the storyboard that the writers constantly revised week to week, patching plot holes and character arcs. Even more impressive was that this mind meld was open for anyone to see—actors, producers, set designers, you name it.

This felt vulnerable to me, the idea that everything was on display, if only because my television roles were never worked out in front of a live audience. I mean, sure, decisions were sometimes altered based on directors' notes, but my home and the trailer were safe spaces in which to try out new options. The writers' space was the opposite, like a public open-faced sandwich. This did not mean, of course, that actors could just wander in there and tell the writers any wacky idea that sprouted in their mind, something like, "Ya know, guys, I really don't like where you decided to put my character in episode five. He should be on vacation in Muncie, not St. Barts. If you could make that change, that'd be swell." You'd have to be deranged to do something like that.

Still, that didn't stop us from trying to sneak glimpses of where storylines were heading. If you were Amy, who had full-blown writing credits on episodes, you likely already knew. That was part of the fun of filming. Despite the open-door policy that existed between writers and actors, a good deal of trust was integral to the preservation of mystery. We trusted that the writers would lead our characters to new, unforeseen, and exciting places, while they trusted that we'd do their writing justice.

As a producer, writer, director, and actor on the show, Amy had as much input as she wanted. Often in Hollywood, the "star" will get producer credit as part of the negotiations but will do little more than the acting part. In Amy's case, she was the real deal. Her writing background gave her the ability to provide informed, smart decisions on ideas being pitched. And as she was also an actor, by which I mean one of "us," she'd have our backs should we have any issues with the script—though that was something she didn't need to do since we had such great relationships with the writers ourselves. Before we shot season 5, episode 5, "Halloween Surprise," she checked to see if I was okay with the Jerry content. You know the one, where Jerry has a "fart attack." It was sweet of her to check in with me, but there were very few things the writers could conceive that would upset me. I trusted them to the ends of the earth.

Greg Daniels

The thing about *The Office* was that we shot in the writers' rooms. When it was time to look out the window, we had a replica of Michael's office, which was one of the writers' rooms that we shot out of. We used the actual parking lot of our offices for the parking lot scenes. The question was how to get production value in a mockumentary because we were doing it for less money than a normal show and we needed to have improvisational ability to shoot in all directions and write a new scene and go out to shoot it. I was concerned that if we were shooting *Parks* on a soundstage in Radford, then we wouldn't have had that ability. It was a boring industrial lot. And the exterior for the government building was at Pasadena city hall, which was very far away and would've been a big effort to shoot there. We needed to have that flexibility as well as have that outdoor space.

A big part of the pilot was the courtyard, for instance. We used to have pigeons. And rain. It was our way of having something that we could control outdoors, which wouldn't look the same as the other scenes. We owned that soundstage through all our seasons, and each season we'd build more and more on it. It was a gigantic set.

Trust was not always synonymous with funniness though, at least if you were a writer. "There's always a *funnier* bit," writer Greg Levine told me. "Something funnier to add. The question is this: how much time are you going to devote to it? How much can you?" Greg's observation has stuck with me. Like actors, writers can get caught in an endless loop of trying to find a better choice for a line or character arc. At some point, we have to go with our gut and move on. I wish I'd had that piece of knowledge decades ago. It would have saved me hours and hours of internal strife. Greg contends that a show like *Parks* doesn't work solely for its humor but for the spaces in between. He and other writers knew that their characters were dynamic due to a combination of laugh-out-loud comedy/joke-writing and *veritas*, i.e., being truthful to what a character needs and wants at the time. In the case of "The Comeback Kid," my decision to make Jerry eager to be Leslie's choice for campaign manager was my version of the "space between the lines." If you were a writer trying to find these spaces, you were helped by the numerous writing assistants who stalked the hallways all day and whose tasks were to take notes and then make connections between what's translating inside the writers' heads and what's working rhythmically and sonically aloud. The writer of the episode would always be with us on set for the shoot, present to help punch up bits that weren't working or to help us if something just wasn't feeling right. They knew the episode inside and out but were also happy to have us pitch ideas on set between takes. No egos. Everyone trying and vying for the best product.

Greg Levine

We had a file on our computer called "Writer Dogs," where we imagined each writer as a breed of dog. Once we got familiar with a writer, the natural next question was: what kind of dog would *you* be? We always had fun like that. It was part of the method to the madness within *Parks*. Sometimes you're writing and sometimes you're coming up with writer dogs.

Oh, and early on . . . we seriously debated whether our main character should be named Leslie Knope. "Is our main character actually going to have the last name Knope?" Greg or Mike asked. We talked about other possibilities, but for some reason every alternative for a last name also started with "Kn." We were obsessed with "Kn." Leslie Knives. Leslie Knowledge.

Fortunately, we were used to having our own shadows in the form of stand-ins, or people (sometimes actors) who looked like us and shared our build and skin tone and who were used by the crew to get lighting and blocking just right. I say that they're sometimes actors because Amy's stand-in, a congenial woman named Hadley, was more than content to work with Amy for blocking purposes and never had any acting ambitions of her own. But for the most part, stand-ins on this show, and others I've worked on for that matter, were typically actors attempting to climb the Hollywood ropes by getting as close to the talent and producers as possible. Arguably, there's nothing closer than being a principal actor's stand-in. This is in contrast to, say, the life of an extra, who is often relegated to long days, minimal pay, crappy take-out food (though on *Parks* the extras had access to the good stuff), and poor exposure to cast and crew. Oh . . . and brutal heat.

Case in point: When I first moved to Los Angeles in 1994, I booked a pilot and a movie, *Ed*, in the first few months, which made things seem promising, much more than they should have for someone in his early thirties. *Ed* starred Matt LeBlanc, in the early days of his *Friends* stardom, and had major production value associated with it. What I didn't realize at the time was that this movie would be a *major* commercial flop that, as of this writing, has a 6 percent Tomatometer score on Rotten Tomatoes. I didn't think such a score was possible, but the proof is there for anyone with an interest in finding out, which I hope is nobody. Anyway, I'd been hired to play Matt LeBlanc's girlfriend's brother, an announcer for the local baseball team of which Matt LeBlanc and one of his teammates, a chimpanzee, are the stars. Let me repeat that so you understand me clearly: *this movie is about a pitcher who's traded to a minor league team and discovers that the star player on the team is a chimpanzee named Ed.*

I was far too distracted to realize what a steaming pile of monkey crap this movie was since we were shooting inside a constructed baseball stadium in Santa Clara, California, in the middle of summer, where it was one hundred degrees and climbing. I was less concerned about myself than I was the extras, who were cordoned off by a rope and given boxed fried chicken lunches, sweating for endless hours as they awaited their slivers of stardom. If that's not bad enough, the character of Ed (aka the chimp) was played by multiple little people who had to take turns donning the costume and running around bases in the flailing manner of our primate brethren. I could've cried watching this madness.

You see, even back then, in my salad days of acting, I had developed a sensibility and compassion for extras. Maybe it was the fact that I'd been one myself not long before that movie and recalled the long, arduous days. I recalled the FOMO associated with wanting so badly to be among the "talent" and convincing myself that maybe, someday, I would. In that humid, sweaty mess of a stadium in Santa Clara, I felt like I wasn't so far removed from those extras eating their "sad sack lunches." But in retrospect, maybe they didn't have it *so* bad. After all, they didn't have to take ownership of—sorry in advance, Matt—one of the worst movies I've ever seen.

Here's how the *Ed* saga ended. When the credits began to roll at the premiere, I swear to God I heard silence for ten seconds before the audience started obligatorily clapping. The kind of applause where you internalize what the heck you just watched before being slapped back to planet Earth. Where what you've seen is so atrocious that people like your friends and family feel like they have to say something, because saying nothing will feel like a bigger crime. Reluctantly, I went up to Matt LeBlanc to offer him my own version of restrained congratulations. "What did you think?" I asked. I expected him to take me aside, throw me a change of clothes, and ask me to join him in a daring escape in which we'd flee through the bathroom window, never to be seen again. Instead, he smiled wide and proudly said, "Jim, I think we have a winner."

Matt saying that made me think that maybe my instincts were

wrong. *This is Matt LeBlanc from* Friends, *and he certainly knows more about the "biz" than I do. Maybe this little monkey film is too smart for us Neanderthals to appreciate. Maybe this will be the beginning of a franchise. Maybe I'll be signing a contract for the next three installments . . .* Not!

Matt got the best revenge of all, though. He returned to the international sensation that was *Friends* and I had to explain to future casting directors that I was in a chimpanzee movie about baseball. When I was fortunate enough to do a guest bit on the final season of *Friends* in 2004, Matt was a true host and pal as he walked me around the set and introduced me to Rachel, Ross, Monica, etc. (at least that's what I called them in my head). More than his bigheartedness, I appreciated his wit as he introduced me to his fellow stars with, "Everybody, this is Jim O'Heir. He was in my shitty movie *Ed*." I spent the week with the *Friends* cast and remember being jealous of what a great gift they had. A wonderful show with people who acted like true family. Little did I know that would also be in the cards for me years later.

As an actor, you're never sure of what's going to hit and what's going to sink. The fun thing about being on a network show though, with an ensemble cast, is that your performance is not measured in one fell swoop but as a sum of many parts. There are episodes viewers don't like (and there are episodes actors don't like either), but they are never enough to diminish the excitement of having made the show, over many years, in the first place. Plus, when you're on a hit show, you start to get recognized as your character more than your actual identity.

By the middle of *Parks*' run, it felt like we were doing all kinds of public events, such as 2011's PaleyFest LA, where the entire cast (and good ol' Greg and Mike) banded together for a long conversation. Panel discussions ranged from figuring out the tone of the show—Aziz makes the comparison to *Seinfeld*, calling it "way different than what it became"—to Greg Daniels directing Chris and Aubrey in a scene, in which Greg remembers Chris wanting to "pound her with Pratt charm." Pratt laughs at the double entendre and wryly says, "That didn't happen." When I think back on this and how lucky I was to sit with my friends and idols on this regarded stage, I'm reminded of just how funny it was to be on a stage with *so* many people. So many of us that the camera could barely squeeze half of us into the frame. How many shows can you say that about? That *Parks* was a show in which you wanted to interview every single cast member? During that same interview, the cast was asked who our favorite fictional character is as well as our favorite character we've ever played. Aziz hysterically answered for Amy, saying RoboCop for fictional and Leslie Knope for the favorite one she's played. But Amy did one better when she admitted that, yes, Leslie Knope is her favorite character she's ever played. Ever.

You see, going back to my earlier point, when you have a character like Leslie Knope who's so popular that even Amy Poehler adores her, public outings require answering for yourself as well as for the character you've inhabited. It's hard enough being one person, let alone two!

I find it very sweet when people tell me that Jerry is their favorite character. But I also find it endearing when someone recognizes me but doesn't know my real name. I can see them searching their phones because they think it wouldn't be cool to call me Jerry instead of Jim. I happily answer to either.

Pratt has told me that he has an interesting interaction with the public, and with fans specifically. "If they recognize me from the *Parks* days," he told me recently, "they make sure to let me know. They're like, 'Hey, I know you from *Parks*,' that it's not *Guardians* or *Jurassic World* or any of these other things. They're like, 'Dude, I'm an original fan. I know you. Not the fake you that you're pretending to be. I know you're Andy.'"

All this affection for our characters showed up in the work, if Rotten Tomatoes is any indication. Season 4 of *Parks* holds a 100 percent rating, nearly the polar opposite of *Ed*. Not bad.

Some of the cast and crew at LA's PaleyFest with many of our smiling fans.

None of us ever got along.

Meet My Wife . . . She's a Supermodel

When I first "met" Christie Brinkley, she was in a poster wearing a red bikini, and I was mystified by the beauty of one of the world's most renowned supermodels. When I met her again, it was real-life Christie, as if walking through the poster and onto the set, twenty years older but not an iota less charming or beautiful. It was hard not to be mystified this time, too.

The idea of Christie Brinkley playing Gayle Gergich was first proposed to me by Mike Schur, who, shortly following the table read of "Ron and Diane," asked me what I thought of a Christie Brinkley type coming in to guest-star as my wife.

"Ugh, I'm not so sure that's a good idea, Mike," I said.

Hold up. I'm kidding you, obviously. What I actually said was, "Oh, bring it on!"

Mike's talent as a writer has always blown me away. He can start off with a premise and then sprinkle in the most bizarre or absurd or wholly original addition. It wasn't enough that Jerry had a wife and a fun backstory—no, he needed a *hot* wife and *three* beautiful daughters. Mike was never afraid of pushing the envelope, and neither was Amy. Upon Mike's introduction of Gayle Gergich's character, she did not hold back. She maybe went a step further in pitching the idea of Gayle being a tiny, chain-smoking waif who's afraid of Jerry returning from the office each night. Jerry is so put-upon by the office and his colleagues, Amy explained, that he has no choice but to take it out on poor li'l Gayle at home. He's so victimized by Tom and April that he releases his anger on the only person he thinks he can control. You don't need me to tell you that this is a terrible idea. Shocking and unsettling, yes. But good? No way. If Amy, Mike, and Greg had gone with it, I would've been the first to protest. The audience would've never forgiven Jerry for verbally abusing his wife. Nor would I. Still, I can't help but laugh at Amy's bizarrely brilliant mind.

I only heard about Amy's pitch for Gayle after Christie Brinkley had agreed to come aboard, which made this idea seem even wackier. Christie is no chain-smoking waif, thank goodness. She's one of the most stunning, self-confident people I've ever met. For this reason alone, I thought it was crazy for Christie to play Gayle. What were they trying to do—give Jerry a fart attack?

Reaching out to celebrities such as Christie Brinkley is usually a pie-in-the-sky endeavor. The show has boasted many celebrity cameos over the years—Jon Hamm, Kristen Bell, Chris Bosh, Joe Biden, Justin Theroux, Bill Murray, and freaking Michelle Obama, just to name a few!—but their appearances usually came down to three criteria: scheduling, familiarity with our show, and *a crap load* of luck. For instance, getting Bill Murray, who appeared in season 7, seemed next to impossible, and if I remember correctly, it was Aubrey who reached out to him to play Mayor Gunderson. It's widely known that Bill Murray doesn't work with agents or managers, so getting a script in front of him is a herculean feat in itself. I don't know what magic Aubrey used, but she convinced Bill to come and play. When the day arrived for Bill to come to set, we all knew there was a 50/50 chance of his showing up. The studio even had different contracts drafted because a traditional deal hadn't been established. As the day wore on and still he hadn't shown, I felt sad that I wouldn't get to meet one of my icons. While I've been blessed to work with some awesome top-notch, A-list talent in my career, Murray is in a category all his own.

Just when I'd given up hope, I looked up toward the main door to the bullpen, and there he was. Bill Murray in the flesh. The guy from *Caddyshack*, *Ghostbusters*, *Stripes*, *Scrooged*, and a million other films. The winner for me was his genius work on *SNL*. Now he was on set, and I was two seconds from doing a repeat of my MTM experience. But some divine creature had given me a breath of confidence—maybe it was the years of being in similar positions with other celebrities—and this time I was able to tell him that I'd worked with his brother Joel and sister-in-law Eliza Coyle over the years and that I thought they were awesome. He was funny, kind, and I'm sure aware of my nervousness. He also ended up being an amazing Mayor Gunderson (God rest his soul), which led to the storyline of Jerry becoming the interim mayor of Pawnee. For the die-hard fans out there, you know how that turned out.

But back to the beautiful Christie Brinkley showing up for season 5 and all of us, especially me, wondering how that would develop. She wasn't familiar with our show at all, I'd come to find out. It was her thirteen-year-old daughter, Sailor, who, upon learning that her mother had been asked by Mike to join the show, told her she needed to do it. Christie later said that Sailor's enthusiasm put a little bug in her head, but it wasn't until Sailor learned that her mom would be playing Jerry's wife that her daughter insisted—*demanded*—she say yes. It turned out that Sailor, smart young preteen that she was at the time, had an ulterior motive: she wanted a chance to visit the set and meet all of us, and Christie was her way in. Sure enough, Sailor was in tow during each of the four episodes Christie did with us. While she took pleasure in getting to meet some of her TV friends, we reveled in getting to make her laugh. What I don't think she understood at the time is that we were just as (if not more) excited to meet and work with her mother. Sailor's excitement was an indication that *Parks* wasn't just connecting with the millennial audience who had first come to *The Office* but with a younger one as well.

Christie was the first supermodel to say yes to us (Heidi Klum would cameo in an episode the following season), which begged this necessary question: why in the world is she married to Jerry? Now, I realize that this setup is part and parcel of the situational comedy that Greg and Mike are experts at—not dissimilar from situations like Ann tending to Chris's hypochondriacal self in season 3's "Flu Season." Situational comedy, in Mike and Greg's eyes, was about character development as much as it was about forwarding the plot, but, in this case, whose character was being developed? And whose was the butt of the joke?

The easy answer is Jerry, who is the butt of so many jokes, including my own. (Remember cube butt?) But I'd like to provide an alternative answer: the fact Jerry Gergich is married to a drop-dead-gorgeous woman—who nonetheless loves and adores him!—makes me think that the actual joke is on his colleagues. It's as if Mike dropped an "I'll show you . . ." on Jerry's office mates, who, though fond of him, can't help but endlessly tease him. But Gayle is another notch on Jerry's belt, as are his three beautiful children.

The audience might've been surprised in season 4 to see a beautiful woman in the form of Jerry's daughter, Millicent Gergich (played by Sarah Wright), but imagine their astonishment when Christie Brinkley stepped into frame. Maybe the lesson for the audience was the same as that for Jerry's colleagues: never judge a book by its cover.*

Before we get back to Christie Brinkley, allow me to briefly

---

* I realize that by describing Christie's beauty in contrast to Jerry's ordinariness, I am ignoring this vital lesson myself. But what can I say? I'm shallow.

mention Sarah Wright, who helped me explore Jerry's naive patriarchal side. Jerry's so supportive of Millicent's independence and femininity that he does everything in his power not to address Chris's creepy comments about her, even when Chris casually utters them to Jerry. Here's a perfect example from season 4, episode 13, "Bowling for Votes":

JERRY: Well, anyway, tonight we are gonna spice things up with a little competition. Whoever raises the most money by the end of the night will win two free movie passes to the Pawnee monoplex.

APRIL: You really think that's gonna motivate people . . .

CHRIS: Oh my God. I could use that for a romantic night with Millicent Gergich. Out of my way, suckers.

There are numerous examples of Chris telling Jerry that he essentially wants to "date" his daughter, and Jerry's lack of a response to them feels like a big, fat "so what" shrug.

Christie Brinkley and I had a riot poking fun at our characters' physical pairing. Which gets us back to the first time I met Christie. She was refined, funny, smart, a wee bit nervous, and ever curious. Remember, the cast had been filming the show for nearly five years by this point and we were so used to one another that we could predict one another's lunch orders. Though Christie had had her share of time in front of a camera, filming a television show and playing into a dynamic of multiple personalities is an entirely different skill set. But Christie was such a pro and never hesitated to ask any of us, including her on-screen husband, for advice on delivery, blocking, and so on.

Christie is also a pop culture idol. If you don't know much about her, suffice it to say she's lived an amazing, glamorous, and dramatic life. Not only has she been through the thick of it with media scrutiny, but she has reemerged more powerful and resolute after tragedy. I can't imagine what it would be like to have gone through what she has—the details of which I don't wish to rehash for fear of playing into the media trap—and to exist as the smiling, ever-positive person I've come to love. Amy would often say that Christie's smile lit up the entire room, but I would add that it lit up the entire house.

But back then, when we first met, her beauty and status were overwhelming, to the extent that I thought it was crazy that someone who looked like her would be "married" to someone who looked like me. Yet again, it seemed like the ugly, two-headed monster of anxiety reared up. This supposed mismatch ratcheted it as high as it had been that time in eighth grade when I danced with Carol Hamilton at the holiday party. Carol and I'd been chosen to play Mr. and Mrs. Claus, and as we shared a dance in the middle of the floor, surrounded by what seemed like hundreds of prying teenage eyes, I felt bad that someone as pretty as Carol had to dance with someone like me. I know all of this sounds melodramatic, but my issues with weight and self-confidence stemmed from my adolescent years and cropped back up whenever someone like Christie Brinkley came around. It was as if the beauty and confidence she radiated were Agent Orange to my self-esteem. Of course, my self-doubt was also an illusion, a story I told myself and regurgitated out of self-sabotage and habit. It couldn't have been further from reality and what others thought about me.

How do I know this? After spotting Christie across the sound-stage on our first day of shooting, I watched as she finished a conversation and sprinted over, her wide, cavity-free smile leading the way. When we were within two feet of each other, Christie embraced me in one of the warmest hugs I've ever been a party to, but it was what she said next that made me giddy. "My husband!" she screamed, and then gave me another big hug as well as a kiss on my cheek. Ahhhh, my Mrs. Gergich.

At that moment, all the insecurity I'd had about our fictional on-screen romance melted off. If Christie Brinkley was excited to play Gayle Gergich, then, damn it, I would be head-over-heels to play her Jerry.*

I learned to appreciate Jerry and Gayle's physically mismatched relationship, and I leaned into the disparities. Christie and I joked about possible Jerry-Gayle storylines, including one where Jerry and Gayle visit the British royal family. Leaving Pawnee (other than their annual trip to Muncie, Indiana) wouldn't be something

I'm much more nervous than I appear. It's Christie Brinkley, damn it!

they'd be familiar with. Gayle and Jerry wouldn't know what the hell was going on, and all kinds of Jerry mishaps would happen.

---

* For what it's worth, as this anecdote likely proves, little Carol back in middle school was probably just as content dancing with me and playing Mrs. Claus to my Santa. At the very least, I hid my fear well!

Of course, Jerry would have some sort of gastrointestinal attack when bowing to the queen. The thought of them with the royal family and all the hoopla accompanying that cracked us up.

When a celebrity gets brought in for a guest spot—be it for a day or for various episodes over several seasons, such as was the case with Christie—the producers make it work. With Christie, we didn't worry about her not fitting into the character, but we were a bit concerned about whether she'd remember her lines and play into the tone that the writers, directors, and producers hoped for. Our *Parks* family was patient and respectful, coaching her through her lines one at a time. Remember earlier when I said that talking heads were one of the most anxiety-inducing parts of the show—even for us trained actors? I'll never forget the day Christie and I did one together. By this time, in season 7, I had come to appreciate the flexibility of talking heads and began to revel in them like I had improv classes at Second City in my twenties. I could detect Christie's anxiety, though. At one point, just as she was finding her rhythm, one of the directors came in with a novel idea. I say this sarcastically. "Christie, why don't you say this?" he asked, and provided several new directions for dialogue—this after we'd gone through many run-throughs of the original dialogue. One of the writers, the brilliant Aisha Muharrar, who was seated next to the director, whispered, "No no, please, we have enough lines." When I realized that we could all have a laugh about this, Christie included, I ceased having a minor panic attack. Christie always gave it 100 percent.

When we weren't filming, Christie regaled me (and many of the cast and crew) with stories of her incredible Hollywood life, which rivaled Rob Lowe's and sometimes exceeded them. Beyond Amy Poehler, Rob Lowe was probably the most famous and storied person on set . . . that is, until Christie arrived. Once

I've obviously loosened up a little.

A Gergich family Christmas.

she did, it was like a marathon story session commenced, in which he and she traded off highlights of their unforgettable experiences. On one of Christie's last days of shooting, there was a line of crew guys who wanted to take pics with her. I had never seen that happen on our set before. We had many famous people come and go, but this was different. Christie, like Bill Murray, is iconic.

Another iconic meeting happened for me that season when I worked with Lucy Lawless, who played Diane, first introduced in "How a Bill Becomes a Law." She'd go on to do ten episodes with us. Not only was Lucy one of my first celebrity crushes— anyone who has seen *Xena: Warrior Princess* likely shares this view—but she was as witty and charming in real life as I imagined she'd be. Lucy is a trained actor, someone who has been in film and television since she was very young. So I was stunned when I was about to get into my car one day after work and she asked a favor of me. "I'm auditioning for a comedy pilot," she said sweetly, "and . . . and I like your work. Would you consider going through my sides with me, if you have time?"

Gasp. Little victories like this one go a long way. "Lucy, I'd be honored," I replied.

The two of us sat in my car for about a half hour and went over her choices for the scene. That's one of those moments in life where you look around and think, *Am I really sitting in my car next to Lucy Lawless and giving her notes on her audition material? Surreal.* I had this same exact feeling a few years later when I was recurring on ABC's *Bless This Mess.* One of the stars was Pam Grier. Yes, *that* Pam Grier. Foxy Brown, baby! I had stopped by set to pick something up as she was heading back to the shoot location, and I asked if she wanted a ride—perhaps I was feeling myself in my BMW convertible. She accepted. In what world does Pam Grier sit next to me as I drive on some studio back lot? Not a world I ever thought I'd live in.

It was nice to hobnob with celebrities, not to mention be respected by them, as with Lucy Lawless. We all want some validation, whether we admit it or not. And by "validation," I mean awards. That includes our show. What I still don't understand is that despite sixteen Emmy nominations over all our years, we garnered zero wins. That's zero wins for Amy. Zero wins for the series. And worse, zero nominations for my boy Nick. I'm not even talking wins now, just nominations. That blows my mind, gets my goat, rattles my cage. The fact that Nick Offerman was never *nominated* for Ron f'ing Swanson makes me question the whole Emmys setup (not to mention the Screen Actors Guild Awards). My costars on *Parks* all deserved recognition, but Nick not getting recognized made me crazy.[*]

---

[*] I am so happy to report that at the January 2024 Emmys, Nick Offerman won Outstanding Guest Actor in a Drama Series for his role on *The Last of Us.* It was a groundbreaking performance.

The first Emmy ceremony we attended as a cast, in 2011, was a swift reminder of how much I detested award shows and, generally, red-carpet events. The shows themselves are fun, but the media fanfare and star-idolizing flattery has always made my skin crawl. You'll see interviewers asking you a question and turning away as you answer, in search of someone who's better and more popular in their opinion. The whole thing can be embarrassing. If I were Tom Cruise or Scarlett Johansson, perhaps I'd feel differently, but I am who I am. Isn't that enough?

What I loved, though? Gifting suites. In case you don't know, gifting suites are lounges where nominated actors and presenters walk away with tons of free swag, compliments of the brands who pay thousands of dollars to be part of these suites. The expectation being that an actor will pose for a photo with their products, be seen wearing or using them, that kind of thing. Who doesn't like free stuff? When the rest of the cast decided to skip the gifting parties, Retta and I were outspoken about attending them. "Fuck that," I remember Retta telling me one year, "I'm getting mine!" Over the years I've received trips, watches, drones, clothing, meals, spa treatments, sunglasses, makeup, gaming equipment, and an unlimited gift card to Johnny Rockets for a year. Retta was right—why not get some free stuff if we weren't getting any Emmys?

It's not like we didn't expect to win, though. We always held out a little hope, or at least I did. At the 2015 Emmys, which our hilarious friend Andy Samberg was hosting, we were seated quite a distance away from the main stage. To my eyes, any seat in any part of the Microsoft Theater was a good one, and there was no shortage of A-listers on each side of us, but it took Nick Offerman all of five seconds to tell us, "These are not winners' seats." Nick had accompanied Megan Mullally to the Emmys so many times (she's been nominated eight times, winning two) that he assessed we were too far from the stage to have the possibility of winning. By the time we'd even gotten to the stage to accept an award (we were nominated for Outstanding Comedy Series that year), the ceremony would've been over, the finale music playing. When it turned out we didn't win, Nick, unironically, returned our sullen expressions with one of remorse. *Sorry*, it seemed to say, *this is why I don't get my hopes up.*

Though we never won, it gave us an excuse to hang out together. There was the time when Mindy Kaling approached me and joked that we had stolen Mike Schur from *The Office*. There was the time at one of the Emmy afterparties—though I forget which year—where John Krasinski and his wife, Emily Blunt, complimented my performance, a top-ten accolade for me. And there was 2015 itself, where, unbeknownst to the rest of the *Parks* cast, I had filmed a promo spoofing the show *Mad Men* with Samberg. I'd gotten to know Andy when he guest-starred as the loud and obnoxious Carl Lorthner (another brilliant name from our amazing writers) for "Park Safety" in season 2. I couldn't believe that five years earlier I'd been worried I'd be chucked from the show after one or two episodes. Now I was doing gags with that year's Emmys host.

Fun as the Emmys were, though, nothing beat the Golden Globes. First things first: when you get to the Globes' auditorium, you're greeted by . . . a big bottle of champagne on the table. I mean BIG. Suffice it to say that while I don't remember much about the 2014 show, I remember a few things clearly. In order of appearance, here they are:

Amy for the win at the 2014 Golden Globes.

- Retta going straight for the big-ass champagne bottle.
- Helen Mirren approaching our table and telling Nick she'd had a dream about him (random but noteworthy).
- Retta, after having drunk said champagne and other spirits, going to the bathroom and missing Amy's win and acceptance speech.

My first Golden Globes. It didn't disappoint.

In her book, Retta tells this amazing story about experiencing a mild blackout and not remembering when Robert Redford tripped over her foot. I had to tell her this after the fact. I also politely told her that if a Mack truck had run over her foot, she wouldn't have remembered.

My embarrassment? In quick succession, I got to meet Glenn

Close and Meryl Streep, who passed me within minutes of each other. They were as gracious as could be and stopped to chat with me after I said hello. You know who didn't stop? Julia Roberts. Perhaps, after seeing me approach Glenn and Meryl, respectively, she said to herself, *Oh hell no, I see what you did with the other two.* And then . . . there was the shit talking. No, not from Julia but from me. During the ceremony, I was caught on camera saying something not so kind about a very famous sitcom star. I hadn't even realized the cameras were on me until my sister texted, **Jim, we can read your lips! Oh, and we can see you rolling your eyes.**

Like I said, the Globes are way more fun.

Perhaps the most significant event of the fifth season was when Rob Lowe taught me how to kiss. Okay, get your minds out of the gutter. Not how to kiss in real life but how to kiss on-screen, and not with each other. As you know, Rob has had more than his fair share of love scenes on camera. And I'm speaking out of complete jealousy when I say that it should be noted that he's also had more than his fair share off camera, but I digress.

One day on set, Rob and I were swapping stories when I asked him what the unwritten rules were when kissing on-screen. As a "big-boned" actor, I don't often get chosen for the love scenes. I don't get the make-out sessions. I'm not cast as the romantic lead with the beautiful wife whom he brings to bed and elevates to unbridled levels of ecstasy. Nope. I'm lucky to get a peck on the cheek. Rob, always happy to oblige, went into detail about kissing on-screen, telling me that, initially, you keep your mouth closed when you go in for the kiss. When your lips meet, it's all up to your scene partner. If she parts her lips, then you can follow suit. If she slips in a little tongue, then you can go ahead and say hello with yours. Basically, it's whatever your scene partner is comfortable with. This advice came in handy when, after *Parks* ended, I got my first lead in a film where I was also one half of the romantic partnership. The film was called *Middle Man*, written by my friend and brilliant writer Ned Crowley, whom I started my comedy career with many years earlier. It's a dark, funny film and the lead character is the anti-Jerry, which was more than okay with me since, after such a long run on a single show, I knew I wanted to take a shot at a tonally different script. The beautiful actress Anne Dudek was on the receiving end of my character's affections, and she ended up in the back seat of a '57 Chevy with me on top of her for an hour while we shot my first-ever love scene. Here's the problem, though: I can declare here and now that while kissing this beautiful woman, all I could think about was Rob Lowe. About everything he had told me. About his open-lip guidance. Of course, doing a love scene on camera is exactly like what you might have heard. It's mechanical, because you must worry about camera angles, lighting, and performance. Not to mention the fact that there were about twenty people surrounding us. Even with all the distractions it was nice for once to be the love interest sweating in the back seat of the Chevy. Even if I was thinking about Rob while doing it.

You might have heard of another kiss I had, with a certain Aubrey Plaza. But that's for another chapter. DON'T SKIP AHEAD. You'll get to it soon enough.

A
Proposal, a
Cancellation

Jerry and Gayle's relationship wasn't the only one having its moment in season 5. You also had Tom and Ann (though that wouldn't last), Ron and Diane, and our sweet Leslie engaged to be married! I couldn't believe it! As Greg Levine recently told me, "*Parks* was a series about relationships, this being the backbone of almost everything we watch as viewers." So I guess you could say this was the backbone in action.

One thing I love about Leslie and Ben's relationship is that it wasn't stuck in some purgatorial will-they-won't-they question, leading up to, say, a final season, by which time the tension has grown stale. Unlike other shows that exploit this trope, the writers and producers had the *doughnuts* to decide they should be together. If the viewers liked the idea—and how could you not?—then why not make it so forever? Forever-ever.

It was just as delightful when the writers put April and Andy together . . . forever-ever. I can remember being on set the day we shot their wedding episode and being so caught up in their fictional emotional journey that I began to cry. In the real world, we might've looked at these two crazy kids and thought they were nuts. *They're too young, it's too soon, they're too immature.* But on TV, Andy and April made sense. Perfect, stupid sense. Their chemistry was also outrageously contagious.

Conversely, Leslie and Ben's proposal scene at the end of season 5's "Leslie and Ben" caught me off guard. Even though I'd read the script and thought they were a strong match, I didn't think they had the exuberance of April and Andy, unchecked as it may sometimes seem. A strong couple, sure, but a passionate couple? Perhaps not. That all changed with the proposal scene, which some critics called one of "the greatest on *Parks and Rec-*

reation." (The other they call "the greatest" is the scene in "One Last Ride" where Ben and Leslie meet then–vice president Joe Biden.)

Amy and Adam had done a lot of work behind the scenes to prepare for this reveal, including, I later learned, keeping away from each other for the entire day prior to shooting. Most people associate Method acting with De Niro's *Raging Bull* or anything Daniel Day-Lewis has ever done, but not series television. Especially not a hit network show. But Amy and Adam's approach was a form of Method acting that increased the tension and mild awkwardness the viewer sees on-screen. And those two ingredients—tension and mild awkwardness—are the base ingredients of what makes Ben and Leslie's romance so pure. The empty house, the idea that the real estate agent is somewhere in the vicinity, the prolonged time that Ben is on his knees awaiting Leslie's answer? All of it coalesces into a geeky love potion that Ben and Leslie sip and pass on to the audience. Amy's and Adam's acting is at a master-class level in that scene, particularly Amy's reaction when Adam walks in the room.

In an interview, Mike Schur said the proposal scene was written with the understanding that the show would be canceled, which might be why it carried so much emotional weight. The writing was fantastic. Leslie first says, "No, no, no. Hold on. I need another second, please. I need to remember every little thing about how perfect my life is at this exact moment."

I've mentioned how in between seasons, we were always anticipating getting canceled. Even though we signed six-year contracts for the show, the executives had the power to cancel our contracts at will. *All* our contracts. There was even a group text where Mike Schur and Amy would update on us on anything they might've heard about us getting canceled or, God willing, renewed.

Mr. and Mrs. Leslie Knope.

Between takes at the wedding of the century.

But there was a time when we were *actually* canceled. Amy told me that somewhere near the end of season 4, the network's VIPs were on a plane from New York to Los Angeles, and on that flight, *Parks* was pulled from the NBC schedule. By the time that plane landed, however, *Parks* was back on. Apparently, a change of ownership at NBC caused this blip, but whatever the actual cause, I'm glad I didn't know about it at the time. Otherwise, I would've been more of a nervous wreck than I already was.

But persevere we did, and thank God for that, because Ben and Leslie's wedding is perfect. Plus, Jerry gets to officiate the wedding up until the point that Tom comes in with the "I do"s. Because of that episode I've been asked to marry people from all over the world. I've been offered first-class flights and accommodations (not to mention a ton of cash) to fly to places like Sydney, Australia, and London, England, to officiate strangers' weddings. I haven't accepted, though I have officiated a few weddings for family and friends. Leslie and Ben's wedding felt a bit like the real wedding of people that I loved and cared about. In the episode, the Parks Department celebrated with food and booze and were all overserved. Feels like that would've happened at a real-life wedding, too.

Morgan Sackett

There were so many crew members on that show that I wanted to keep working. I felt a responsibility. Every year there was some new show that was "going to take us down." *30 Rock* was on in the beginning, but then there was *Outsourced* and *Community.* We had shot a handful of episodes in season 2 and very much felt like we were on the fence, and Amy came to set and told us she was pregnant. Remember, we shot twenty-four episodes, took two weeks off, and shot six more. Like thirty in a row, while Amy was quite pregnant. The first episode post-pregnancy was "Harvest Festival," and by the time we got to that spring, there was a plane ride to New York where we were told that we were canceled. But the only reason we weren't really canceled was because we'd already made those six episodes. If we hadn't made those six episodes, we were over.

Greg Daniels

If I remember the ratings for *Parks* off the bat, I think we did pretty well. A lot of times I would prepare the ground for discussion with the networks and say, "You know, a lot of the time, great shows don't start off right." I'd say, "Remember *The Office*? They did blah blah blah." And when I was doing *The Office*, I'd say, "Remember *Seinfeld*? Remember *Mary Tyler Moore*?" Also another very low-rated show off the bat. *Cheers*? Any time you do something unusual, you're not going to get good ratings in the very beginning. Also, you're not going to get good focus-group results. Focus groups at that time tended to interpret it as "You're asking me to tell you what a TV show is, so I'll tell you what it is based on everything I can gather from what's on the air, so if something is different I'll react to it as not being a TV show, as it being something else." The downside to being cautiously optimistic is that, like when I was doing *The Office* and kept comparing the start to *Seinfeld*, they told me they were giving me five episodes to start. "That's one more than *Seinfeld*," they said. "We only gave him four."

If you think about if *Parks* had aired on Netflix, I don't think they'd have had any issue about bringing it back for season 2.

In those days there was a lot of jockeying for a limited amount of slots. You keep *Parks* on, that means you have to tell Bonnie and Terry Turner (huge TV producers back in the day), or whoever else, that they can't be put on. So, looking back on it, you're not necessarily as comfortable as it might appear.

If romance in Leslie's life soared during season 5, instances in Amy's personal life had shifted, and it soon became apparent that she and her husband, Will Arnett, were splitting up. There were a few trickles of rumors here and there, the kind you ignore because they are distracting and not conducive to the work being done on set, but they soon became impossible to ignore. Gossip functions like that: a seed germinates into a potted plant that one day explodes at the roots and takes control of a city, Jumanji-style. The paparazzi hanging around set fed this growth.

One day, Amy came up to me between sets and said, "Jim, you might start hearing stuff about me and Will." I asked if everyone was okay (meaning nobody sick or injured), and she said, "I'm fine, the kids are fine, Will is fine." Being the softie I am, I told her to let me know if there was anything she needed. I couldn't imagine going through a big life event while having to lead a prime-time network TV show. The pressure must have been heartbreaking at times, yet she showed up every day with a smile on her face.

Like all of us, Amy wasn't thrilled when personal drama and work mixed. This is not to say she disliked the idea of the personal and professional ever mixing but that she was wary of unnecessary drama affecting the mood we'd worked so hard to preserve on set. As a longtime star and powerful person in the industry, Amy had been a witness to how paparazzi can wreck one's self-esteem and even destroy lives.

Like the time Amy and I were shooting a scene in a park. We were standing on a podium when she noticed that paparazzi had made it onto the set, hiding themselves under a car to avoid being caught. These camera critters would do anything for a potential scoop.

"I don't believe it," I said to Amy as we watched one camera-person scamper from the car.

She looked unfazed. "It is what it is," she said. Part of me wanted to protect her from the cameras and publicity, but again, it was Amy who did the protecting. "I'll get them out of here," she added, and called security. As I said, in her mind, distractions plus drama equaled an unhappy set.

There were so many distractions caused by shutter-happy paparazzi over the years, some of which made me plain sick. Reporters and camera crews would follow around Pratt and his then-wife, Anna Faris, whenever they went to visit their son, Jack, who was in the hospital's NICU for a few weeks after his birth. There are some lines you just don't cross, and a couple's sick newborn child is one of them. I can't imagine the extra stress this must've caused Pratt and Anna, both of whom were already in a vulnerable position.

Chris Pratt

Amy was such a great number one, and she always cared about our well-being. It was a hard time for us—[Jack] was in the ICU for a month. And Amy would check in on me— she'd have a code word she'd say to check in on me. She was someone I could turn to and talk to.

If there are perks to not being a mega-famous star, not being followed by paparazzi must be at the top of that list.*

Fans, however, were always welcome. When we went to Indianapolis to shoot the season 5 episode "Two Parties," the one where Leslie and Ben celebrate their respective bachelorette and bachelor parties, we were greeted by hundreds of screaming fans. It wasn't just for Rob Lowe this time either. It was for all of us guys, since the scenes we were shooting were centered around Ben's bachelor party in Indy and the gals didn't accompany us. When the blogs and the local papers picked up on the fact we were filming there for a week, so did the *Parks* fans. Their obsessiveness didn't disappoint.

Indianapolis is like *The Office*'s Scranton, a real place in addition to a TV show setting. Also like Scranton, Indianapolis regarded itself as an underdog, as a place in which people lived and not where, shall we say, culture came to thrive. This is not a knock on "the Hoosier City"—I'm Midwest born and bred and lived on the Illinois/Indiana border for the first twenty-five years of my life. This is to say that movie stars and musicians and painters don't necessarily flock to the Midwest to find work and sustain their craft; they go to New York and Los Angeles and Atlanta. So, when it became clear that *Parks* was proudly touting its Indiana connection, that it didn't view it as some sort of sarcastic punch line made by Tom Haverford but was making an earnest tribute, its residents responded in kind. And they responded loudly!

While taking a break in the trailer during filming one day, I heard several voices pitched above the rest, leading a group into

---

* Though, if you're reading this, *Us Weekly*, I'm available any time you want to photograph me carrying a latte after leaving the mall . . . I mean the gym.

what I could only make out as a chant. I stepped outside to see if I could interpret what was being said. That's when the rumble increased to a roar, contained within it a name: "Jerry . . . Jerry . . . Jerry." And there it rolled along until it quickened its pace, "Jerry, Jerry, Jerry," like I had just scored the winning touchdown in the Super Bowl. It was, I thought, a beautiful melody.

I poked my head out of the trailer like a groundhog and heard even more applause and shouts. They wanted Jerry to come out, and they wanted him now.

"Jerry, Jerry, Jerry!"

"Uhhhhhh, hello!" I finally uttered. This was an improvement after Mary Tyler Moore. "How ARE you?!" I shouted.

"We're GOOD," the crowd screamed back.

And so on and so forth.

Shortly after, one of our producers, Doug Smith, asked me, "Have you ever had that happen in your life?" Doug was genuinely struck by it, too, despite his years being on sets and around crowds of all sizes. Maybe he saw how much it had surprised me, how blown away by it I was.

"Never," I told Doug. "That was . . ." *Pause.* "My Beatles moment."

I know how ridiculous it is to compare a Jerry chant to perhaps the most famous band the world will ever see, but that was how it felt whenever we went to Indianapolis. If the cast were the Beatles in some alternate universe, then I was the Mal Evans to their Paul, John, George, and Ringo—the ever-reliable and hilarious roadie. But Indy was our Liverpool, it was our Scranton, it was our Cincinnati. (I needed to get a *WKRP* reference in here somehow. The Thanksgiving episode with the flying turkeys kills me to this day.)

We were having a blast in Indianapolis, and our time at Lucas Oil Stadium, where the Colts play, was no exception. What fans don't see in the charming smiles of quarterback Andrew Luck and wide receiver Reggie Wayne is us six dudes running around and making complete fools of ourselves for about two hours. As several of the crew set up for that afternoon's filming, the six of us ran around the field (a hundred yards is long when you're out of shape!) and drew up pretend plays. Now, I was never the greatest athlete, but I was no slouch either. As a bigger dude throughout most of my life, I've prided myself on my ability to use my size to my advantage. I wouldn't be drafted to any D-1 teams, heck no, but I could show up, have some fun, and be competitive.

At one point, Luck, who had a cameo in the episode, began throwing us balls, and even his softest throws were harder than any I'd tried to catch. (I think the only one of us who made a catch was Pratt, a bomb from Luck that made it into the final cut.)

After warming up with some balls—*heyoooo*—we decided to attempt field goals. We set the ball up at the ten-yard line, and one of us held the ball while another attempted a kick. You know how fans get irate when kickers miss extra points in the NFL? Not me any longer! After trying a bunch of times in an empty stadium and barely lifting the ball fifteen feet into the air, I have a ton of respect for those kickers, who make it look simple.

There was somebody who made the kick, not just once but twice, and his name is Chris "Renaissance Man" Pratt. At this point in that handsome devil's career, you could tell me that Pratt will be competing in the 2024 Summer Olympics pole vault and I'd believe you. But back then, he was still our rookie of the year—young and inexperienced but ambitious and with so much

Why so serious? We were gearing up for a game that afternoon.

Andrew Luck, a talented quarterback and a wonderfully sweet man.

Andrew Luck, me, and Reggie Wayne. One of us is not a pro football player.

to prove. Even Pratt himself didn't know he could transform into the human fitness machine he's since turned into. That dude was the biggest eater I've ever seen (and I'm a big eater myself). Let me give you an example: Remember the episode in which the Parks Department tries to lift Tom's spirits by taking him (at Jerry's recommendation, shockingly!) to a dinosaur-themed restaurant called Jurassic Fork (season 2, episode 11, "Tom's Divorce")? That scene took several hours to shoot and required us to eat food. By "food," I mean plates of barbecued glazed ribs. When filming scenes where eating is required, actors usually take small bites of their food, remembering the additional takes required to shoot. Often, there will be spit buckets placed nearby to help control portions, which I'd learned about during my first experience eating on-screen, for the Comedy Central show *Strip Mall*, in which my character was supposed to eat a Krispy Kreme doughnut. One doughnut over many, many takes. I decided, however, that my character was going to eat a full doughnut during *each* take. I learned a valuable lesson that day . . . upchuck into one of those buckets, but away from your costars. If you really want to see me in action with food, check out my *Better Call Saul* episode in the final season. Cinnabons for days!

But Pratt ignored the unwritten "small portions" rule while filming "Tom's Divorce." While Aubrey and Aziz were snacking on seaweed wafers—I know they're trendy but *YUCK!*—Pratt was living on his own pig farm, taking down rack after rack of ribs. After all that food, he still asked what they were serving for lunch on set. Turns out, though, he's not superhuman after all. "I was absolutely sick," he told me recently. "I was doing it for the attention and to get a rise out of people. For entertainment value. To shock."

Pratt had to suppress this ravenous appetite once he started getting bigger roles that required him to get in shape; *Moneyball* was the first one that boosted his fitness regimen. He'd film with us all day and dash to the gym after, or he'd wake up at the crack of dawn to work out with a trainer prior to coming to the soundstage. Within a relatively short time, Pratt had transformed from that adorable, slightly soft version of Andy whose visage you likely summon when you think of *Parks* to the toned image of perfection that creeps into episodes from time to time. But as quickly as Pratt snapped himself into shape, he put the weight back on, like a Jekyll and Hyde of nutrition. The reason being, quite simply, that Pratt liked to eat. It wasn't a secret—he was proud of this fact. We had some pretty good catering on the show, and he and I were never shy about enjoying it. During season 4, after Pratt had filmed *Zero Dark Thirty*, he told me that he received a call from the film's producers saying that a reshoot of one of his scenes was required. This is standard fare in the movie world, but months had passed after official filming for *Zero* had wrapped . . . and Pratt had put back on his weight.

"Shit, man," he said. "What am I gonna do? I'm supposed to be a SEAL, and now I'm a . . ." He patted his belly. Then he fell to the ground and started doing push-ups. It turned out that it was a reshoot in a helicopter where Pratt's character was to be seated and in fatigues, which meant there'd be no full shots of his physique. I told Chris at the time that as you get older, the game of losing weight isn't going to be so easy. Age has a way of changing all that. He was still at the point where he could work his ass off and get back into shape quickly. Since he became a perfect physical specimen for *Guardians of the Galaxy*, he's kept himself in great shape.

A few years ago, when Pratt hosted *SNL*, some of the cast and I flew out to surprise Chris and celebrate this rarefied honor. We sat in the front row as he delivered the monologue in which he admitted to his fluctuations in weight over the years, joking that he was on a dietary program where a studio offers you big money to do a film so you have to "stop being fat." We went into a laughing fit over that one, but he was also shining a light on the sad state of the entertainment industry, where calories are constantly counted, pounds are weighed, and one's image is always subjected to scrutiny. That Pratt was able to acknowledge this fact while staying true to himself is a testament to his maturity at such a young age. Pratt has transformed into the Terminator in recent years, but whenever we're together his love for food fills me with bountiful joy . . . though we still haven't returned to that restaurant that gave me the runs all those years before.

All this talk about food, besides making me hungry, gets us back to Indianapolis and the shoot of a lifetime. It also scratched the nostalgic itch that had been itchy since Rob Lowe joined us back in season 2. In season 5, episode 10, there's a scene in which we eat at the steakhouse St. Elmo's Fire, which, of course, is a tribute to the eighties classic that Lowe starred in. It happens to also be one of my favorite movies. In the *Parks* episode, as our characters are nearing the entrance, Rob pays a funny little homage to the movie that helped catapult his career. It's a small physical movement, something you'd miss if you took your eyes off the screen for a second (and I urge you to go back and find it), but it's a perfect metaphor for the marriage of my eighties youth and career arc, a reminder that never in a million years did I think my life would intersect with Rob freaking Lowe. Much as Rob was paying this tongue-in-cheek homage, I, too, was honoring this coincidence.

Unfortunately, not everything about that St. Elmo's episode was worth remembering, like the unexpected appearance of Newt Gingrich. I have no idea if he knew we were there or if it was just a coincidence. (I think most politicians have never met a camera they didn't like.) Either way, he was on set and Mike Schur decided to throw a cameo appearance his way. I have to be honest, I wasn't thrilled, since I'm not a fan of Newt or his politics, but I trusted Mike and knew he was always thinking about what's best for the show.

In the scene Mike wrote, Jerry and Tom accidentally sit at Newt's table, and Jerry tells Newt they might be related because their last names are so similar. Newt responds, "I don't think so, Jerry." As usual with *Parks*, the bit was smart and funny. That being said . . . I still didn't like it. My problem with Newt's appearance on the show was that nothing about his personality or politics reflected the communal—dare I say, democratic—spirit of *Parks*. Everything about him seemed to suggest it's his way or the highway.

We were usually given the following week's shooting script a day in advance of the table read, but because our writers were often under the gun to finish, there were times we didn't get the draft until right before. I always looked forward to seeing what my involvement would be—some episodes my role would be heavier (no pun intended), and some a bit lighter. Plus, the scripts constantly blew me away. Week after week, season after season, they got stronger. I credit that to the fact that not only did we have some of the smartest and most talented writers in the biz, but also Mike Schur never left us. A lot of times when a writer has a hit show, they'll get opportunities to move on to other projects they've created. That could've easily happened with Mike. He cocreated, along with writing genius Dan Goor, *Brooklyn Nine-Nine*. Mike could've left to run that show, but instead Dan took those reins and Mike stayed with us. We never lost his voice. Of course, we missed Dan. Watching him work on set when we needed to change a line or come up with a new bit was magical.

Which brings us to the terrifying moment in season 5 when I thought my time at *Parks* was coming to an early end. It was one of those days where a production assistant dropped off the script just before the table read. I hate to read a script cold at the table, so I knew I was going to have to review it quickly. I wasn't too worried, though . . . until I saw the title: "Jerry's Retirement."

WTF?!?!

Now I've been in this business for almost a million years and have heard all sorts of crazy stories about how people have been let go from shows. Some saw it on the news. Some showed up to find their parking space was gone. I even heard a story where an actor found out they were let go from their series regular role when the guard on the lot wouldn't let them in.[*]

I sat down and started to read the script, my heart racing faster and faster. There was every indication that this was it for good ol' Jerry:

JERRY, *holding a box:* Well, everybody, um . . . wow . . . it has been an honor and a pleasure to work with you all. The time I have spent at Parks and Rec have been the happiest days

---

[*] Damn, that's COLD!

of my life here in the government. (*Everyone looks confused.*) And I know everyone says it, but I sincerely hope that we always stay in touch. (*Everyone is silent with confusion.*)

LESLIE: . . .What the f**k is happening right now?

JERRY: Today is my last day. Leslie, I am retiring.

I was in disbelief. How could they write off my character without telling me in advance? I know shows change and characters come and go, but no warning? I loved these people, and they were sending me out without a heads-up? I kept reading, and it only got worse.

LESLIE: When Jerry first applied to this job, one of his goals was to have a building named after him. Again, that is an absurd request considering your work record. But I thought, maybe he could have a room named after him. So, henceforth, Park and Rec Conference Room will serve as a testament to your years of public service. (*Leslie places on the wall a plaque that says "JERRY GERGICH—MEMORIAL CONFERENCE ROOM 1971–2013 . . . RIP."*)

(The RIP was because the plaque was made at the last minute and the person who made it thought Jerry had died, so the gang ends up saying it meant "Retire in Peace." Yeah, that's definitely better.)

I kid you not, at this point I'd worked up a sweat. I was having a really hard time comprehending what was happening. Normally, I would have run over to Retta to see if she knew anything, but there was no time. The table read was soon, and the script kept getting more and more ominous for Jerry. Leslie even goes over to Jerry's house to apologize for not giving him a better send-off. She brings a scrapbook showing Jerry's years in the Parks Department (it was only four pages), and she realizes after spending time with Jerry's family that all is not as it seems. Jerry has a pretty amazing life and a family who loves and respects him. She even gets to have breakfast with the crazy Gergiches as they sing their morning ritual, "Eggs, Bacon, and Toast."

By the final couple of pages, I'd resigned myself to the fact that this wonderful acting job was coming to an end. Then came the tag at the end of the show.

THANK GOD FOR THE TAG AT THE END OF THE SHOW!

I had to read all the way through the final pages to see that, indeed, Jerry wasn't going anywhere. He would be working part time at the office, which was just a way to explain why I would still be around.[*]

Feeling incredible relief, I pulled myself together and went to the table read. When I walked in and made eye contact with Morgan Sackett and saw the smirk on his face, I knew I had been played. I couldn't help but laugh because they got me. They definitely got me. One of my favorite things in life is busting balls. Well, I had just gotten my balls obliterated.

Ultimately, once I recovered, I couldn't have been more thrilled with this episode. There had been past instances where the office mates got to see that Jerry had a great family life, but this episode let the viewers know why ultimately Jerry didn't care what everyone thought of him at the office . . . or in the world. He

---

[*] Oh, did I mention, THANK GOD FOR THE TAG AT THE END OF THE SHOW!

has his family that he's incredibly proud of and who, as we learn, are also incredibly proud of him. This episode also lets Leslie see that Jerry isn't just a fumbling oaf. You can see this realization in Leslie's face when Jerry is showing her pictures from the Gergich family album, the idea that he has it all. This comes to a physically comedic peak when the Gergich family comes in for a hug and Leslie has to slide her way out. There's only so much Gergich an outsider can take.

I'd been on the show for years by now and felt solid and safe around the cast and crew. I knew they had my back. It was touching to know that the showrunners were trusting me with such an important chapter in the life of one of their creations, who'd also become an extension of me.

Jerry was here to stay. *Parks* was here to stay. And our relationships, well, they were stronger than ever.

The Beginning of the End

Maybe I spoke too soon, because come season 6, two of our biggest stars would leave the show.

It's true: by the middle of the sixth season, Rob Lowe and Rashida Jones (whose characters were married by this point) had exited *Parks*, their "subplot" having taken them to Ann Arbor, Michigan, to live out their lives devoid of governmental bureaucracy. The decision to leave in real life was uniquely Rob and Rashida's—and everybody, including the producers, has confirmed this fact—but I couldn't help but wonder about the possible chain reaction caused by this decision. If season 6 was a wild card of a season—from the crazy number of guest stars to the location changes (London!) to the unexpected merger of Pawnee and Eagleton—it was made wilder and more unpredictable by the hole that Rashida and Rob left.

Let's be honest: when the media reports on these instances and says that a decision is "mutual," they're usually suggesting that it's anything but. Mutual is boring to gossip magazines and blogs. Even "reputable" sources like the *Huffington Post* tried to stir things up, writing in August 2013: "Was the decision for Jones and Lowe to leave the show mutual? Was it due to money? How will Leslie Knope (Amy Poehler) cope with the loss of Ann? Find out below!"

Naturally, my calling out these rags doesn't mean I wasn't curious myself. One of the rumors I'd heard was that Rashida couldn't quite understand why her character would continue to hang around the department season after season when Ann didn't work there. Yes, she's Leslie's bestie, and yeah, everyone adores sweet Ann, and yeah, she's usually the logical antidote to the department's chaotic habit of dicking around, but maybe Rashida's point was also valid (if it did exist). I can think of many long-running shows that have forced their characters into situations that are nonsensical, and even great shows are sometimes riddled with problems of longevity, with plotlines and character tropes running dry. I'm not saying I felt that way about our show (or that anyone did—our reviews were better than ever!), but if Rashida had wished for different choices for her character, then I can understand her thinking. Or maybe, just maybe, she'd grown tired of playing Ann for multiple seasons. Bob Denver, who played Gilligan on *Gilligan's Island*, once said that nobody could ever see him as any character but the guy in the silly hat. I don't think Rashida or Rob would've suffered the same fate as Bob Denver, but this fear rings true. I, for one, wondered if I'd always be seen as Jerry. Was that a bad thing? What would Bob Denver say about that?[*]

Mike Schur

Rashida came to me before that season and said she had gotten an offer from Pixar to be one of their writers. She said, "I really want to do this; I want to get more into writing, and this is a wonderful opportunity." She was going to begin work on what became *Toy Story 4*. The way that those jobs work is that you have to go up there, and you live there for two years and you are part of this kind of artist collective where you have a main project that you are working on and you are also helping other people with their projects. That was her passion at the time. I love her endlessly and always want her to be happy, and I was

---

[*] Bob Denver is a smart man, it turns out. He also said this in an interview: "I like to take a puff or two before going on the air. I still get stage fright when I have to perform. A little grass gets rid of the problem." For me, a swig of Diet Coke and sharing a laugh with Retta or Chris would do the trick.

like, "You got it." Part of our ethos in the writers' room, too, was that if you are a writer and you are also a stand-up, and you have a stand-up gig, go do a stand-up gig. If you are an actor and you get an opportunity to do a part in a movie that is going to take you out for three days, go do it; we'll work around it.

It kind of perfectly coincided, as we started to talk about that season. That story, which I really liked, has a natural ending, which is that Ann and Chris stay together, get married (or don't, who cares), but they have a child, and they leave and go somewhere else. We had also said that Ann was from Michigan; I don't know why. I think it's because I was born in Michigan; I have a fondness for Michigan. I was like, they should just get married and move to Michigan to be closer to her family. It was again one of those things that seemed kind of charmed when you look back on it. We weren't planning on writing them off the show, but when she said she wanted to leave, the path went in concert with the storyline that was already going on. We had all this advance notice, which is great because those things only seem jarring when the writers can't plan for them. We were able to slowly lay in this story where she and Chris Traeger got closer and closer, and then eventually she goes on a trip to Bloomington with April because April is looking at graduate schools.

Then we were sort of thinking it also leads to wonderful stories for Leslie, because Ann was kind of a booster rocket that helped Leslie become the person she was becoming. Now, we would be in a situation where Leslie would have to be on her own. She wouldn't have her security blanket, her best friend, her support system. In the sixth season of a show, you need to change things; you can't get caught in this stasis and never move forward. We talked to Rob and told him that this was our plan, and he totally got it. We wrote that nice ten-episode send-off for Ann and Chris, and there are a lot of different ways that actors leave shows. Ninety-nine percent of them are bad, with some kind of conflict or unpleasant situation, or some kind of lawsuit is filed or whatever. It's a testament to the show that the way two of the main actors ended up leaving was by hugging and crying and laughing and celebrating and thinking, *This was great; this worked out well.* Everyone is happy, and they are sailing off into the sunset.

As much as I hated to admit it, I thought Rob and Rashida's departure signified the beginning of the end. I say "the beginning" because I knew we still had a lot of fruit punch in the juice

This was a tough day. We said our goodbyes to Rashida and Rob.

box, but there was something that made me worried about being viewed as too long in the tooth. (Am I overextending metaphors here?) We'd lasted six seasons by this point, far longer than anyone thought we would, including our showrunners. I was so afraid of our show not being liked any longer that I convinced myself that

One of the last days with all the boys. Nick is even kind of smiling here.

Rob and Rashida knew something about our future that we ourselves didn't. Though that would all prove to be self-conscious, internal actor babble, it felt authentic and significant at the time.

Mike Schur

We started to really feel around then that we were nearing the end. After season 6, Amy and I had this tradition where the writers would get together, usually in June, and we would work on the new season and then I would call her in mid-July. She used to go to Nantucket (and she might still) with her family. We would set up a time, and I would call her and walk her through the idea for the season—the big major arcs and the character stuff—and she would go out and sit on the beach and look at the ocean. I would talk for an hour, she would give her feedback, and we would go back and forth. It was kind of this lovely tradition that we established. That year, after season 6, I said we need to talk now, before July. I told her my gut says that we should go to NBC and tell them that we want season 7 to be the last season. I think we have this opportunity now to call our own shot and say we think creatively this show is coming to an end; it feels right.

We had a big idea for the last season, which was that we were going to jump ahead in time and do the whole season in the future. Before season 6 even really ended, we talked to NBC and said we think that next season should be our last season. They said, "We totally get it, awesome; go with God." The last wonderful thing creatively that happened was that we were able to go into our final season having decided *ourselves* that it was the final season.

Best waffle topper? Whipped cream. We were each given our own can.

They tell you in therapy that feelings aren't real or that feelings aren't facts or something along those lines, but I'm here to tell you that they're as real as you believe them to be. And I'm known to have a wild imagination! If you're rational, you channel these fears into your acting and performance, but if you're irrational like I am, you convince yourself of the worst. Like my experience with *Logan Lucky*.

In 2015, I was in Kansas City doing a play at the amazing New Theatre when I received a call

Is it waffles? Is it a cake? It's both!

asking if I'd like to audition for the Steven Soderbergh film, starring Channing Tatum, or "Chan" as I'm fond of calling him. (It also starred Daniel Craig, Adam Driver, and Hilary Swank.)

I was a giant fan of Soderbergh, not to mention that this invitation to audition was the biggest call I'd ever received. When opportunities like that come along, you seize them. These were the pre-tape days, when actors were expected to come into town to audition, but since I was in Kansas City and unable to travel due to an eight-show-a-week schedule, the casting director asked if I could put something together on video (which is a much more common thing today). I shot it in my dressing room (with fellow actor Craig Benton Stout), sent off the tape, and thought nothing of it. A couple weeks later I got a call saying that I had booked the part, some of the happiest news I'd ever received. In addition to this information, I was told that the part required I perfect a "very specific" Southern accent and that I would be linked up with the dialogue coach who'd been working with the rest of the cast. This accent seemed to be a big deal, too, because this was repeated to me several times. *It must be very specific.*

Within days of accepting the job, I was sent video and audio clips that demonstrated the type of "very specific" Southern dialect the producers wanted me to do, which increased my fears since the people demonstrating were, according to the casting director, experts at doing very specific accents. Furthermore, this accent was *hard*. No matter how many ways I recorded myself doing it, I sounded nothing like the examples in the recordings. This failure was confirmed when I got on the phone with my dialect coach, who told me that I wasn't even in the right town, never mind the right ballpark. I told them I'd do the best I could—what else can you do except say that, really? My efforts reached their fated low point when the dialect coach said emphatically, "Channing has gotten the accent down. He's killing it." As if I needed more proof that Chan is great. "But don't worry," she added, "you'll get it, too."

Flash forward to a couple weeks later, when it was finally time to go to Atlanta to begin filming. There I was, thirty thousand feet in the air, script in hand, and having a full-blown panic attack. I'm not joking: cold sweats, an elephant on my chest, my face as pale as a urinal. I looked so distraught that one of the flight attendants checked on me several times, likely convinced I was seriously ill. The reason for my surprise attack? I'd convinced myself that due to my inability to get the very specific accent down, my casting in *Logan Lucky* was one giant mistake.

Not only that, but I'd been given the role by accident and Soderbergh, upon seeing me, would send me back on the next outbound flight. *Soderbergh had never wanted me*, I thought.

I pored over lines in the script, as if focusing on something besides my mental status would help. It didn't. Each line echoed that I was *not* the person for this role.

I made it to Atlanta in one piece and had calmed myself down enough to appear presentable for hair and makeup the following day. Once inside my trailer, I had the pleasure of meeting the oh-so-wonderful dialect coach face-to-face. Once again, she couldn't help boasting of Chan's language achievements. "He's nailing it," she told me. "Channing has it *down*! He's blowing me away . . . How are your lines coming along?" Well, they weren't coming along at all, because every time we ran through my part, she stopped to correct me. While I had enough willpower to stave off another panic attack, I was utterly confident that I wasn't giving them anything they needed. Short of Soderbergh meeting me face-to-face and firing me on the spot, I had made my bed.

The twenty-four-hour period that followed proved to be among the hardest of my entire life, which I realize is a super-privileged thing to say. But I'll say it anyway: that anticipation terrorized me. It was made worse when I learned, on day one of shooting, that Steven Soderbergh—the man, the myth, the job incinerator—wanted to see me. Hey, at least I could be put out of my misery.

"Jim!" Soderbergh cried, bringing me into his embrace. "How were your travels?"

Huh? This was not the welcome I'd expected, but his conge-

Chan and me, taking a selfie to send to our buddy Pratt.

niality taught me everything I needed to know, which was this: I was an idiot who had imagined a firing because I didn't have enough self-belief. Not only did Steven know exactly who I was, but he was excited to see me. All that self-doubt about my being cast by mistake, about my not being worthy of acting in a Soderbergh film, about my not being able to hold my own in a film with huge stars, was extinguished by his gigantic warmth.

But wait, there was still the matter of the accent. "Steven," I said, "I want to let you know that I'm doing everything I can to get the accent down, and I just hope that it's okay. I'm trying, I'm giving it my all."

Without a moment's thought, Soderbergh said, "I don't give a shit about the accent," before changing the subject.

If you think that's funny, imagine my surprise when I got to meet Channing on set and learned that not only did he not have the very specific accent down, but the one he did have sounded *exactly* like mine—a very typical and not-very-specific Southern accent. And if you think my accent was lackluster, take a listen to Englishman Daniel Craig's in *Logan Lucky*. (I love you, Daniel.)

Still, I wasn't convinced I was in the clear. When we were shooting and it appeared that Soderbergh was giving me very few acting notes, I told myself that it was because he thought of me as a lost cause. Even when things are going well, the brain will find reasons to believe otherwise. I was so nervous about the lack of notes that I went up to Chan between takes. "I'm a little worried Steven isn't giving me any notes," I told him.

He smirked and said, "That means you're giving him exactly what he wants. You're doing it right."

I've been on hundreds of sets over the years. I know that when a director isn't giving you notes, it's usually because he's confident in your performance. Usually. But because I'm a neurotic actor, I figured this was that rare time when notes weren't being given because he didn't think I could execute them. Believe me, folks, it isn't easy being me.

Oh, and one more thing: when filming *Logan Lucky*, I learned that Channing Tatum and I shared a friend in Chris Pratt. Imagine that—Channing Tatum and I having anything in common, though it turned out we did. Channing and Chris got to be such great friends that their families would go on beach vacations together—talk about a hot-boy summer! By the time the shoot was done, I had settled in and enjoyed the experience, even drinking vodka with Hilary Swank and Steven Soderbergh. I'd tell you about it, but I don't remember.

Now, dear reader, you've been presented with two different versions of Jim O'Heir. In the first, you have a self-conscious and confused actor who refuses to take credit when things go well and blames himself when things don't. In the second, you have someone so delusional that he'd risk safety and dignity (yet again) for a chance to do what he loves. This is the duality of the acting life—there's no other way I'd have it.

This dual mindset was temporarily assuaged when, prior to the airing of season 6's "Anniversaries" to our millions of viewers, the producers sat us down in a conference room before our weekly table read to tell us they'd made changes to the opening credits. *Changes?* One of the producers clicked on the conference room TV and the credits began to roll, the chirpy patriotism of the melody mixing with the rolling snares, a theme we'd heard a thousand times and that I enjoy to this day. Just when my patience was fading, I witnessed one of the most humbling visuals: my name, Jim O'Heir, in the opening credits sequence, followed by Retta's. I'd barely registered what was happening when the room erupted into shouts and hoorays. Soon, I found myself locking eyes with Retta, caught in that paralyzing joy that such visuals bring about. We were in the opening credits. We'd finally made it!

I have to say I never put much thought into the fact that Retta and I weren't in the opening credits. I always thought it would be nice, but I wasn't pissed about it, as the kids say. There's only so much time for the opening credits, and every second counts. A sitcom isn't a full thirty minutes. It's under twenty-two minutes, after commercials. Any time lent to opening credits took running time away from the show, and so what if my name wasn't in the credits? What mattered was that I was in the show. My girl Retta has a different take.

Retta

Jim can speak for himself—I was pissed! We were added during, what, season 6? I hate that I have salty feelings about not being included on a show that I'd been on for *six seasons*, especially when there were people who started after me who were on the opening credits. But whatever, I have my love of being included on my first regular gig . . . but are you kidding me?

Seriously, though, it was exciting. But . . .

It would've been more exciting if it had occurred during season 3!

Plus . . . they used footage of me that I didn't like!

UGH.

It was symbolic that this credit unveiling occurred during "Anniversaries" (episode 14), which shows the fraught relationship between the towns of Pawnee and Eagleton after a merger has united them but has not made their respective residents happy. Meanwhile, Ben plans to celebrate his and Leslie's one-year anniversary, but his plan backfires and results in his inviting Jerry to do all the couple's anticipated activities with him instead. It was a Jerry-heavy episode, with a chance to bring Jerry and Ben together. They hadn't had a storyline involving just the two of them up to this point.

Some days on set are easier than others.

Adam Scott and I had to take dance lessons to prepare for one of the scenes in "Anniversaries," where I learned that he—perhaps due to his size and weight and age—was much lighter on his feet than I. We had a lot of laughs getting through the scene, which we barely did. Here are two guys who aren't professional dancers by any stretch of the imagination and we're in each other's arms ballroom dancing. We also had to figure out who was going to lead, which was a bit of a battle as we were both vying for it. Goes without saying, but I won that battle. During one of the takes, when we were kind of dancing across the floor, I heard a *pop* and then felt a sharp pain rip through my calf muscle. Adam also heard the pop. "Was that you?" he asked. "I hope it wasn't me!" It was me, but at that point there wasn't much we could do about it. We still had to shoot the rest of the scene. I muscled my way through it and ended up on crutches for a couple of weeks after due to a knee injury. Adam Scott told me recently that the word "hero" gets thrown around a lot, but on that day, I was one. Whether it's a gastrointestinal crisis, a knee injury, or a potential heart episode (read on), the show comes first.

This reminds me of the time I was working on my first show as a series regular, *Strip Mall*, which also starred Julie Brown. One day, Julie and I were filming a scene that takes place in a restaurant booth. During one of the takes, I started getting chest pains. At first I didn't think much of it, but as the day continued the pains were getting worse and worse. I was terrified, but as it was my first regular gig, I had no intention of screwing up the shot or the day's schedule. That mindset was so stupid when I look back on it. I could've been having a major heart event. After we wrapped, I drove myself over to the emergency room in Burbank, where I was admitted rapidly and urgently. I think when an emergency room sees a fat guy come in with chest pains, they take it seriously. Thankfully, it was nothing more than a panic attack and I was home the next day.

Although Adam and I hadn't spent a lot of time off set together since his coming aboard in season 2, "Anniversaries" awarded us the opportunity to get to know each other and enjoy each other's style. Where I'd observed Adam's humor and casual affect around Nick Offerman, with whom he had Megan Mullally (*Party Down*) in common, I could now play off his easygoing nature while we were shooting the horse-and-buggy ride or, better yet, receiving a couple's massage together. At times I forget that Adam wasn't on the show from the outset. He was such a perfect fit for the role and for the cast.

At the end of that week of filming "Anniversaries" together,

Adam told me that he liked to watch me work. At first, I thought he was in character and saying that as Ben, to which I would've said, "Creepsville!" But when I realized Adam was talking, I took it as one of the best compliments I'd ever gotten. In 2017, when I won a Daytime Emmy for a role I did on *The Bold and the Beautiful*, Adam called to congratulate me. I also heard from the rest of the cast on our Parks Family text chain. They're just a great group of people.

Since I just mentioned my Emmy (there's a sentence I never thought I'd say), this is as good a time as any to tell you how all that went down. After *Parks* wrapped, I started working on all sorts of different film, TV, and theater projects. I love Jerry and will forever be grateful to have been given the chance to portray that lovable, hung oaf, and I was hopeful it would lead to other opportunities.

One of those opportunities was for the soap opera *The Bold and the Beautiful*. They were looking for me to do a cameo duet with Monica Horan from *Everybody Loves Raymond*. (She played Robert's wife, Amy.) They thought the audience would get a kick out of seeing these two familiar TV characters showing up in the fictional town of Port Charles. I'd never done a soap before, but I knew that they shot forty to sixty pages of dialogue in a day, this in contrast to *Parks*, which shot something like thirty in a week. The number of lines and pages was daunting, but I was up for a challenge. And that it was. Monica and I hit it off immediately and had a lot of fun playing Matt and Kieran Cannistra, two travelers who somehow keep finding themselves on flights with a few of the regular characters. We would end up coming back and ultimately did eight episodes.

Cut to many months after I shot my first few episodes, and it's time for the Daytime Emmys to announce their nominations. To be perfectly honest, the Daytime Emmys were not on my radar. I'm not much of a daytime TV watcher, whether it's for soaps or daytime talk shows. (Although I loved *Maury*.) The morning of the announcement, I was heading to Chicago for an appearance of some sort when I received a call from CBS Studios. I had no idea what it could be about, and normally, I don't pick up unless I know who's on the other end. Like many of us, I learned that lesson the hard way. But since the caller ID said something about CBS, I knew it had to be work related.

"Hi, Jim," came the voice on the other end. "This is Bradley Bell. I wanted to congratulate you on your Emmy nomination."

I was so confused that I thought it was probably one of my buddies pranking me. While Mr. Bell went on to congratulate me and talk about the nomination, I put him on speakerphone so I could start googling the Daytime Emmys to see if it was a bunch of BS. Turns out it wasn't. Go figure.

I wasn't planning on going to the event because some friends of mine were doing a show together for one night only, and I wanted to see it. But I got pressure from the show and network to attend, so I begrudgingly said I would. My publicist found out that my category would be announced around 5:30 p.m., and since I figured I had no shot at winning, I thought I could sneak out afterward and still make the performance. Perfect.

On the day of the awards show, I took my tux out of the closet (it hadn't been used since the last time the *Parks* cast had lost at the nighttime Emmys a couple years earlier—you've already heard that story), slapped on some deodorant, combed my hair, and headed to the Daytime Emmys. I was seated next to some of *The Bold and the Beautiful*'s cast. What struck me as a bit odd was that these seats, unlike the ones the *Parks* cast had at the Emmys, were actually good. They were located a few rows back in the center section; my seat was on the aisle.

My category hit around 5:35 p.m. Larry King and Leeza Gibbons came up and did some banter before reading the nominees for my category. Immediately, camerapeople ran over to where each of the nominees was seated so they could get the reactions when they inevitably won or lost. I was all prepared to give that fake happy look that losing nominees have done since time immemorial.

If I thought I didn't stand a chance before, now I knew for sure I wasn't going home with a trophy. I was blown away by some of these clips. The first was Nichelle Nichols (not only famous for playing Uhura on *Star Trek* but also the first Black woman to have a leading role in a TV series). The clip showed her character dying in a hospital bed as she said goodbye to her son. Tears flowing and all. *Damn, that's your winner*, I thought. Next up was Tobin Bell (famous for the *Saw* film franchise), and he was screaming up a storm. So intense! *No, that's the winner.* This thought process continued when each subsequent clip was shown. Then it was my turn, a comical clip from one of the episodes I'd done. I could barely watch it. These other actors were either screaming or crying (or both), and there I was doing a comedy bit. I tried to shed this embarrassment by peeking at my watch, getting camera-ready for my fake smile.

Larry's famous voice boomed, "The winner is...JIM O'HEIR!" *Pardon?*

It wasn't until the actress sitting next to me started shaking me that I realized it was *my* name that Larry had called. People were clapping and staring at me, and the camera was practically up my nose. I headed to the stage and ascended the stairs, the entire time thinking, *Please don't trip, please don't trip, please don't trip. Fat guy falling up the stairs will definitely make the news.* I was simultaneously reprimanding myself for not having written any type of speech in case I won. But this just wasn't on my radar.

Once I got there, Larry handed me my Emmy (which wasn't the real Emmy . . . they give you that later) and I steeled myself for some sort of acceptance speech. I had about ten seconds to compose my emotions as the claps softened, and I decided that I would just speak from the heart. So, that's what I did. I thanked my reps, family, and friends and then boldly said, "This is for all the soap actors out there." I set the award on the ground, stepped next to the podium, and did an *I'm not worthy*–type bow to my fellow actors in the crowd, my way of showing how much I appreciate their hard work. Soap actors have been given short shrift over the years. Some people don't look at those actors the way they do a nighttime TV or

I won an f-ing Emmy. What?!

film star, but, from my perspective, they work harder than many. I know the material can be formulaic and repetitive, but damn, they make it sound real.

Near-Crimes and Missed-Demeanors

In all my years acting and immersed in the business of watching actors try to sound natural (it's harder than you think!), nobody did this with as much bona fide naturalism as Ben Schwartz, or, as you know him, Jean-Ralphio. I was treated to Ben Schwartz's improvisational genius over twenty episodes over seven seasons, but in season 6, it was his appearance in the first episode, "London: Part 1," that reinforced my admiration. It's during "London" where we also get to meet his father (as well as learn the identity of Tom's business rival . . . here's looking at you, Fonzie). Rewatching Ben Schwartz's appearances, I am most struck by how he makes Tom's freneticism seem almost, dare I say it, normal? That despite how eccentric Tom is, Jean-Ralphio has one over on him. It's hard stuff to pull off, but clever writing and Ben's fantastic performance make it possible. I went crazy whenever I was presented with a call sheet and saw that Ben would be joining us on set for an episode. He was one of the few people who could break us all on set, and that's with legends like Amy and Nick. Ben was able to crack us up every time. There were even spots in the script where the writers had added "Let Ben Schwartz do his thing" because even those icons understood how big of a force he was. You understand how complimentary I am of Amy, Nick, Chris, Retta, Aubrey, Rashida, Adam, Aziz, and Rob—all of whom are pros when it comes to improv gags—but I gotta say it: Ben Schwartz is just a cut above the rest. (Ben, I'll send you my Venmo info shortly.) There are too many amazing moments with Jean-Ralphio to list, so I'm going to drop a few of my favorites here. Remember, you have to imagine Ben Schwartz performing these lines as Jean-Ralphio with his singsongy style . . .

"Did someone just talk about a job opening? Guess who's got two thumbs up and was just cleared of insurance fraud? This guy! Got off on a technicality!"

To Ron Swanson: "Business partner now and forever. Hold up—Forever 21, twenty-one-gun salute, *Salute Your Shorts*, kaboosh! I just free associated all over the moo-stache."

Talking about his sister: "She's the woooooorst!"

"It's like I always say. When life gives you lemons, you sell some of your grandma's jewelry and go clubbing."

Okay, maybe I spoke too soon, because nothing, absolutely nothing, beats Chris Pratt's improvisational gag from season 2, episode 6, which has become legendary among our crew and became infamous when *Bustle* published word of it. There's a scene in this episode where Andy brings flowers to Ann to win her back after he receives what he perceives to be a sexy voicemail from her. The bit called for him to be naked, but in television this always refers to putting on a dance belt or special shorts and shooting from the waist up. You can imagine everyone's surprise—including Amy Poehler's genuine

Such a kind, kind man . . . Henry Winkler is nice, too. ;)

shock, which you see in the final edit—when she opens the door to see that Chris Pratt is indeed very, very naked. Like for-real naked. Moments before the take, Pratt thought it would be funny if he stripped down and surprised Amy and Rashida inside; it was the kind of shenanigans Pratt would pull all the time (especially with humor that borders on shocking). The network and their lawyers didn't find this funny, however. Pratt has told this story on *The Graham Norton Show*, but in case you don't know about it, he received a stern letter from NBC's HR department following his nude stunt that essentially told him he was on probation and that, as he relayed to Graham Norton, "there is protocol about nude scenes." I don't know if there's any truth to the bit that follows, but what I heard happened was a production assistant who got offended that Pratt undressed reported it to her boss, who reported it to another person, and so on down the line. It didn't help that Pratt was so cavalier in his attitude about it in the months that passed, telling *The Graham Norton Show*, "I framed the [HR] letter!" The irony here is that in the scene prior to Pratt's infamous self-pantsing, Leslie calls Andy to say she wants to meet "without lawyers present." When he doesn't return her calls, she pushes forward, in frantic Leslie form, and asks, "Andy, why aren't you calling me back? It's because of your lawyer." Little did Leslie or Andy know that real-life lawyers would soon make themselves known.

If the "naked Pratt" story has become the stuff of behind-the-scenes lore (and can you imagine if that happened today? Photos of his "thing" would be surfacing across social media accounts everywhere), my near–faux pas has lived inside my head . . . until now, that is.

Remember when I told you about season 2's "Park Safety" episode? The one where Jerry falls into the creek and makes up a story about a mugging? Well, in one of my favorite scenes—and the audience's, too—Jerry is giving his version of a PowerPoint presentation and the folks in the office have been told by Leslie to keep it nice. Jerry has been through it, in Leslie's opinion, and she wants everything to go well for him. Of course, their being told to be nice becomes code for "give Jerry subtle digs." (If you need a refresher on the insults, please go look this up on YouTube—it's hilarious!) As with all scenes, we shot multiple takes from multiple angles to make sure there was coverage of each character. While shooting and cracking jokes, I broke the cast more than a few times. Like the moment Jerry was talking about trout season and he bends over, splits his pants, and farts. "I'm done, I'm done," I remember Amy saying. "You can't get me to laugh anymore." *Oh, you're not done yet,* I thought. *Not even close.*

I headed back to wardrobe for my change for the next take with a plan in mind. They had pre-split a number of pants so that when I bent over we would definitely get the tear. Instead of a quick change of pants, I decided that I would also take off my underwear. I knew that if a quick shot of my hairy ass ("Hairy Ass" was going to be my first radio announcer name, by the way) didn't make them go off completely, then nothing would.

On the way back to set, I ran into Lozo (one of our great production assistants) and told him what I had in mind. I said he would probably want to stick close to the monitor in video village (where the director/producers/writers/script supervisors watch each take) so he wouldn't miss the big reveal. Lozo thought my idea was so funny that he wanted to give a heads-up to the folks at video village. That's where things went off the rails. After we heard "action" and began the scene, I also immediately heard "CUT."

Cut? WTF? I was just about to shock the room. The director ran in and asked to talk with me. "Are you wearing any underwear?" he whispered.

I said I wasn't.

"Please do not do this," he warned. "After what happened with Pratt, I think this is looking for trouble."

Busted.

I was disappointed but went back and explained to the cast what my plan was. They laughed, but it wasn't the laugh I knew I could've gotten had I been able to complete my mission. Looking back, I'm glad it played out the way it did. If things had gone as planned, there's a chance the cast and crew might've been given a view of more than just my adorable cheeks.

I know I've called this season the wild card one, but it truly was. If it wasn't the hour-long episodes in London to kick it off (and Rob and Rashida leaving, which proved our emotional low), then it was guest stars in the form of Tatiana Maslany, Heidi Klum, and Michelle Obama in the season's finale. It took Amy doing leaps and hurdles to get the First Lady to appear on the show. (It's not a relaxed job from what I hear.) But Amy and Obama had reached an agreement where Amy would campaign alongside Obama for her "Let's Move" initiative and Obama would cameo in *Parks*, wherein she'd further promote the mission. This was a win in every sense of the word: our show got a huge ratings bump because of the First Lady's appearance, and a great cause benefited from the promotion. Since the Obama cameo occurred in Washington, DC, due to scheduling (and since Obama was already promoting "Let's Move" there), I wasn't able to see one of the coolest First Ladies in our nation's history unfortunately. I had one over on Amy, though. I got to meet Newt.[*]

Beyond the wild array of guest stars that season 6 brought on, we also had some surprise guest directors, Nicole Holofcener being one. Holofcener is an icon of American film direction and is known for her whip-smart dialogue, repeat casting of female actors like Julia Louis-Dreyfus and Catherine Keener, and tasteful blending of comedy and drama, which has made her one of my favorite directors. Take a look at *Enough Said*, or the more recent *You Hurt My Feelings*. The cast, crew, and producers all admired her, which must be why she directed four episodes over the years.[†] Unlike some directors we'd had in the past, who would "apply" for one of these stints, Nicole was recruited. Her affable and skillful direction of season 6's "The Pawnee-Eagleton Tip Off Classic" remains one of my favorites. Another major talent who directed us? Nick Offerman. His directorial debut was season 5's "Correspondents' Lunch," and in season 6, it was "Flu Season 2." I would be remiss if I didn't acknowledge that a fellow actor directing an episode of a show can sometimes be distracting, not to mention a poor choice, and I can list several examples from shows of years past, though of course I won't.[‡]

I was worried that two things would happen when Nick took his seat in the director's chair, and possibly simultaneously. The first was that Nick would be apprehensive about giving us direction, and the second was that we would be resistant to any

---

[*]   Remind me to throw up, please.
[†]   Season 3's "Eagleton," season 4's "Smallest Park," season 5's "Jerry's Retirement" (do you think this is my favorite episode of hers?), and season 6's "The Pawnee-Eagleton Tip Off Classic."
[‡]   Ask me at a Comic-Con and maybe I'll tell you.

direction he was able to give. Remember what I said earlier about actors taking direction from guest directors? I feared that scenario. But Nick, expert actor and humble person that he is, knew each of our characters so well that the direction came off as encouraging as opposed to condescending.

After Nick, I became a fan of actors who end up directing. They know what the actors' concerns are and how to relate. And like most actors, I can become insecure and need affirmation and guidance from directors. There are so many directors who only worry about camera angles and technical stuff, most of which will drive someone like me crazy. Nick took the advice of our amazing DP (director of photography) Tom Magill, who would go on to DP for Rashida's show *Angie Tribeca*, for camera and lighting issues, which freed him up to spend time with us. He was so keyed in that he'd often refer to things our characters did in previous seasons that even we'd forgotten. Most

Foreground, from left to right: Nick Offerman, Mike Schur, and Morgan Sackett. Brawn meets brainpower.

important were the calmness and compassion he brought to the set, especially when it was obvious that so many things on set were changing, even if, by every apparent metric, they were going so well.

Take Pratt. No, no, he wasn't leaving us like Rob and Rashida were, but he was gone for a quarter or so of season 6 due to other filming obligations, by which I mean *Guardians of the Galaxy*. On most sets across film and TV, leaving to take on another role when you have a contractual obligation is a no-no. But not on *Parks*. I'm not going to go as far as to say that taking extra work was encouraged, but it wasn't forbidden. Mike Schur's theory, one he'd repeat to us over the years, was the more that was happening out in the world for us, the better it was for the show. Visibility merits more visibility, or, in other words: *Go out there and be the best guardian you can be, Chris.* I sometimes wonder what would've happened to Pratt's career if he'd been blocked from filming his mega-moment. Would he forever be known as Andy Dwyer? What would have changed? You must remember that Pratt wasn't as well-known back then as he is nowadays, and he'd be the first to tell you that he was twenty to thirty pounds off from becoming a star (the unfortunate framework of Hollywood culture). Beloved as he was as Andy, Chris Pratt at this time was still trapped in the belief that his character could become the rest of his life. Luckily, each of us went on to do many other things after *Parks* (Pratt chief among them), and I attribute this to Mike and Greg's encouragement of our careers. The show wasn't viewed as the sole destination but as another stopover in an actor's journey.

Chris Pratt

I can credit Mike Schur and *Parks* for letting me do *Guardians* because I was under contract to work with them for twenty-something episodes, and *Guardians* was going to shoot during the season—they literally let me out of the show to shoot *Guardians*. They didn't have to do that. The cast and crew even went to London to justify my disappearing.

After twenty-five years in the business, you work with people like Mike and Morgan [Sackett] and Dean [Holland], and you understand how rare it is to have the special gift of folks who are great storytellers and also decent people who care deeply about the well-being of the cast. It was a special chapter in all our lives.

Hey, Marvel, I'm available!

A journey is never a journey without gleeful mementos along the way, and season 6's "Galentine's Day" was one. Yes, it was a reprisal of sorts of season 2, episode 16, "Galentine's Day" (yet again demonstrating the writers' creative show-naming), but it also flipped the script on its head because, well, it had to. You see, Ann, who was such an essential part of the original Galentine's Day, and who served as Leslie's confidante throughout the show, leaves in season 6, which means that Leslie is forced to find a new best friend in the office. To do so, she organizes a brunch with Donna, April, Shauna, Ethel Beavers, and "Fake Ann" (she's grasping at straws, that Leslie), but she receives a call from Real Ann saying she's given birth. Leslie rushes to Ann Arbor, Michigan, to be with Ann, who tells her to be more patient with April and Donna because they would do anything for her. This, my friends, touched my heart. For one thing, it summoned viewers to remember the show's emotional core, how, in the simplest sense, its characters are always trying to be liked rather than respected. In another sense, it provided an opportunity for my lovely Retta to shine . . . and how I love to watch my girl on-screen. "Galentine's Day" reminded me that the character traits that viewers have grown fond of are often hidden in plain sight and need only gen-

I love this funny, talented, beautiful gal.

tle prodding by other characters—in this case, Leslie's misplaced but ultimately harmless need to find a new best friend in Ann's absence. Leslie cannot alter April's dry detachment or Donna's tough love, but she can certainly make viewers see that there's as much love within the office as when Ann was there.

Amy and Rashida's friendship continues to this day, as exemplified by a funny bit they did a couple years ago for *Vanity Fair* where they slapped lie detectors on each other and tried to test each other's loyalties. The first question Rashida asked Amy was whether the rumors are true that a *Parks and Recreation* text chain exists that she's not on. Amy paused before admitting, "Yes." The text chain had been set up after Rashida had left *Parks*, and no one thought to invite her. The day following this bit, Amy texted the group and introduced its newest arrival, Ms. Rashida Jones.

"Galentine's Day" was also a beautiful reminder of how much I missed Rashida—her tranquility, her loyalty to Amy, her devotion to the acting craft. It showed me something else, too: myself. At the end of the episode, when everyone meets to discuss the Unity Concert, Jerry arrives late and is reprimanded by . . . you guessed it: Tom and April. Ben, ever the mediator, comes to Jerry's defense and calls him a good friend, but when he tries to rally the rest of the office to change their unkind stance, he, too, is reprimanded. (Sorry, Ben, I could've told you that would happen.) This scene immortalizes Jerry, because as much as we like to see things progress season to season, there are just some things that cannot—that will not, that should not.

But don't worry, Jerry will get the best of them yet. And no, I didn't see it coming either.

One Helluva Ride

Do you know how people in long-term relationships reach points where they need to reconnect? Spending time with each other, going on dates, planning trips, rediscovering that je ne sais quoi? Heading into season 7, the cast decided to do more get-togethers like those we'd done in seasons past. Maybe we wouldn't attend another one of Rashida's pajama parties as an entire group, but we could try more group hangs. With Rashida and Rob now gone, there was no greater reminder that any of us, at any moment, could leave, to say nothing of the show that had united us in the first place. We have to do this, we told one another, before it's too late. I had always loved the conference room scenes, but now they seemed more precious than ever. And whenever we were all cooped up in the Winnebago on a location shoot, we itched to be even closer.

I suggested earlier that Rob and Rashida's exit portended the end of the show for me, but there were a few people who knew that season 7 would be the end for real. It was at one of these get-togethers at Amy's house that the end was hinted at.

We were sitting around a fire pit in Amy's backyard when Amy came out with advance copies of her new book, *Yes Please*. She handed each of us one and said, "If you guys don't mind, I'd like to do a very Leslie Knope thing and read what I wrote about you in my book." Damn. That got my eyes wet pretty fast. She read with her Leslie Knope–like punchiness softened by Amy's real-life grace. After Amy read Nick's section, I recall Nick turning to us and wiping his eyes. Turns out I wasn't the only one crying. "There must be a lot of pollen in the air," he joked. In fact, I don't think there was a dry eye in the house. Like Amy herself, the words in her book were sincere, lovely, and perfect. Amy's reading to us wasn't a clearly expressed "This is the end"

Huddled in a corner waiting for a flight to Indy.

A series wrap-day selfie for Garry and Ben.

moment, but it felt a little bit like the wind-down at a yoga class. The slowing down of momentum. Of breathing. Of all our irrational thoughts.

We were at another get-together at Nick's when Mike Schur sat us down to say season 7 would be our last. Unlike Amy's delightful tribute, Mike's news was direct and unvarnished. Thirteen more, he said, and that would be it. The fact that Mike had told it to us straight, and to all of us while we sat together, made the jagged news feel easier to handle. *Thirteen more, guys.* Before I tell you about the emotions it unleashed—there were so many tears during this time—allow me first to tell you how beautiful Nick's house is.

Between Nick's *Parks* run and Megan Mullally's *Will & Grace* legacy, NBC had paid a pretty price for their combined star power. And Nick and Megan had earned every penny, and they must've spent most of it on the elevator, the infinity pool, and an outdoor barbecue that was a block long. Nick's party was the envy of any house party I've ever been to before or since. Gorgeousness aside, Nick was also the perfect host, as content partaking in the fun as he was making sure we were enjoying ourselves. A good host should always strive to be less of a standout than the guests, and Nick was that to a T. But Nick was doing what he'd always done ever since I'd met him in 2008. He was just being himself. There's a reason why many people think Los Angeles is full of "fake people" who try too hard to be likable. They're all trying to fit in or to stand out. Nick doesn't try at all.

But when Mike Schur told us that season 7 would be our swan song, any kind of awe I'd experienced while admiring Nick's domain melted away. One moment I was peering at Nick's impressive stairwell, and the next I was flashing back to that first day of the *Parks* meet 'n' greet in Studio City where I was blessed to find people who would become lifelong friends. Time slowed as I peeked around the table and caught the eyes of my castmates—I mean, my friends. And then . . .

The tears started. Oh, how they did. They were a combination of happy and sad, a confusing crossroads in which the destination was the same: the show was ending and there was nothing I could do about it. I fought them back as Mike described possible end scenarios for the show, consoling us with the thought that it would be a majestic and satisfying conclusion to a stellar run.

Between Mike's news and preparing for the end, there was nothing left for us to do except hug one another and promise that, in these waning days, we would see one another as much as possible.

But everyone was so, so busy. What else do you expect from an all-star cast like ours? Amy was finishing her book and preparing for a tour by the time we started filming, while Nick was coming off the bestselling waves of his book *Paddle Your Own Canoe*. When he was writing his book, Nick would retreat to his trailer, where he'd bang out chapters, while I'd go to mine and watch episodes of *Judge Judy* or *Maury*. Please, as if you've never watched *Maury* in the middle of the afternoon! It's literally what America's suburbs have been built on. Good ol' toil and sweat and *Maury*. Anyway . . .

Nick was always invested in some creative project or another, be it his various books or his woodworking business, which was growing in scale and popularity. To say it's just a business reduces his aim and passion—everything he does is with utmost precision, care, and love. For example, when the show ended, Nick removed some doors from the set, made oars out of them, and delivered them to our homes. Retta had all of us sign her oar, and she auctioned it off to raise money for her nephew who was going through a life-threatening illness. (Thankfully, he's doing great.) But contrary to popular belief, Nick's not great at everything, folks. When it comes to baseball, Jimmy-O might have one up on him.

Shortly after *Parks* ended, I was asked to throw out the first pitch at a baseball game in June 2017. In the years since, I've thrown out more first pitches, dropped pucks at hockey games, and performed a number of athletic rituals, but most memorable of all was when I was asked by the Cubs, my hometown Chicago team, to throw the first pitch.

How hard could it be?

If you've ever seen a professional baseball game, then you know the answer is *pretty damn hard!* There are YouTube compilations and news articles devoted to these screwups.[*]

I learned a rule after consulting with many experts and watching videos of these mishaps: *Don't hit the grass.* That's all. It doesn't matter if the ball goes thirty feet upward or to the right, or if it goes so far it hits somebody in the box seats. Any of that would've been acceptable to me. (And hey, MJ missed way, way wide.) But not getting to the dirt around home plate would've been sad.

I had a template for how not to fail, at the very least, and his name was Nick Offerman. Nick was perhaps at the peak of post-*Parks* Ron Swanson fame when he walked out onto Wrigley

---

[*] If you want a quick laugh, watch Dr. Anthony Fauci's or Michael Jordan's pitches. One is an uber-geek and the other is one of the greatest athletes of all time. If Michael Jordan—who threw out a pitch for the Cubs back in 1998—couldn't do it well, what hope did I have?

Field to throw his first pitch a month before I tried it; the chants for Ron were deafening. What the fans might've overlooked is that Nick Offerman is not Ron Swanson. Ron is a meat-loving, likely baseball-idolizing picture of Americana; Nick is a super-talented actor who did not grow up playing baseball.

Nick had thrown the ball so poorly that he even spoofed himself—staging it as a silent movie and sharing that clip in an interview on *Conan O'Brien*. Since Nick's pitch had made some local Chicago news, and even Nick himself found it funny enough to share with Conan's late-night audience, I learned a second lesson from Nick's poor performance: *Whatever you do, don't make the news.* Nick told me that he was heckled upon returning to the stands to watch the Cubs game, which scared me even more. If you know anything about Chicago baseball, you know that Cubs fans are used to being disappointed, but they hope you can at least throw the ball sixty feet. Being heckled by my hometown fans would've haunted me till the end of my days. *Damn it, Jerry, you screwed up the Harvest Festival and now you've ruined the game!*

Okay, so I was standing on the mound at Wrigley Field on the day of my big debut, shocked at how far from home plate I was. When I'd practiced in my yard throwing a ball to my dogs, I'd nailed it every time. Had even measured the exact distance. Now the distance appeared greater, the stakes higher, and the noise louder. That's when a third lesson popped into my brain: *Do better than Nick.* Forget the previous two rules—*Don't hit the grass* and *Don't make the news*—and just focus on this one. *If you can out-man Ron Swanson himself,* I told myself, *then you'll be just fine.*

See? Sometimes April can be nice to Jerry. Whatever my name is.

Hitting the picket line with my boy Nick in support of the SAG-AFTRA strike in 2023.

I released the ball, felt my arm motion propel through time and space and baseball history. My beloved Cubs, my beloved Chicago, my entire life flashing . . .

Do better than Nick, do better than Nick, do better—

The cushioned sound of the ball hitting the catcher's mitt. *Ahhhh.* It wasn't a strike, wasn't even in the vicinity, but it hit the dirt (not the grass) and bounced into the catcher's glove. As far as I was concerned, Jerry had done all right.

Shortly after, as I was watching the game from the stands and rewarding my athletic performance with a jumbo dog and a cold beer, I texted Nick. **Dude, at least I hit the dirt,** I wrote. I felt his LOL and love and slight jealousy pour out from cozy Los Angeles or wherever he was at the time. Whether you were him or a super-athlete like me, we were united in representing our *Parks* family in the very American pastime of baseball.

One more thing about baseball: while it was true that the *Parks* family would never win a championship in the softball fantasy league of ensemble shows, doing signings after throwing out a first pitch was among my favorite outings. They're chock-full of families and young people, and young people—meaning people in their twenties during the show's reign—loved us. I always enjoyed watching an entire dugout's expressions whenever I'd approach and tell them I was a big fan of their team. "No, we're huge fans of you!" they'd respond.

I'm blessed by the exposure *Parks* has given me and thankful to have been steadily employed since. I'll say yes to any job I find inspiring, but the dream scenario occurs when you love the script *and* you discover that it's shooting in a cool location you've never been to. Michael Caine is famous for saying that he chooses projects based on where they're shooting, and I absolutely understand the thinking. There's magic in the perfect script meeting the perfect location. This was the case when I was asked to audition for *Better Call Saul*. Like most people, I'd been obsessed with *Breaking Bad*, which naturally carried over to *Saul*. The audition was for the role of a mall security guard (Frank) who was obsessed with Cinnabon, and the storyline had Saul manipulating the guard with the tasty treat to pull off a heist in the mall. Food, hijinks, and *Better Call Saul*? Count me in! Stars aligned and I got the call telling me that I'd booked the role, but before I could start, I was informed that the director, Michelle MacLaren, wanted to talk to me. Sometimes the director of a film will sit down and discuss the character, but it isn't that common for a TV guest spot. It turned out that Michelle wanted to make sure that I was comfortable with cutting and eating the Cinnabons. There'd be a lot of them, she told me. "Michelle, I was born for this role," I said to her.

Production took place in Albuquerque, New Mexico, a place I hadn't been to but was excited about, given my zeal for *Breaking Bad*. The day I arrived, I was told that I would need to see the hair and makeup department as well as wardrobe. All very standard. The only thing that was a little odd was that the director wanted me to stop by the shooting location to meet her. Michelle and I talked through our thoughts on the character I would be portraying and how to handle the Cinnabon-athon. Then, as I was about to leave, she asked me if I knew who was also on set. I had seen the call sheet for the day, and other than Bob Odenkirk (whom, of course, I loved), I hadn't recognized any of the names. She told me to peek around the corner and look at the person in the electric cart. I did as I was told, and there she was . . . the one . . . the only . . . Carol Burnett. Carol F'ING Burnett. This might not seem like a big deal to some, especially if you're

Meeting Carol Burnett was a dream moment for me.

under forty years old. But to a guy who was glued to CBS on Saturday nights watching *All in the Family*, *The Mary Tyler Moore Show*, and *The Carol Burnett Show*, and made his living in the TV/film comedy world, this was a big deal. The biggest deal. I later learned that the reason I didn't see her on the call sheet was because they were using a fake name to keep it a secret from the public, as she was going to recur on the show during its final season.

When I regained my composure after my initial sighting, Michelle asked if I'd like to meet her. Meet her? She's on par with my love for Mary Tyler Moore . . . and we know how that turned out. But this time I couldn't say no. Wisdom says that you should never meet your heroes, and for many, I'm sure that's true. But Carol was as wonderful, kind, and funny as I dreamed she'd be. And as opposed to my run-in with MTM, I maintained a coherent conversation this time. Instead of hiding my nervousness through ridiculous reticence, I told her how nervous I was to be talking to her. She put me at ease by telling me about when she'd met Cary Grant in her early days and how nervous she had been. We traded stories back and forth until she was ready to shoot her scene, which she performed skillfully, even at the age of eighty-seven. I watched her do a three-hander with Bob Odenkirk and Pat Healy, and she never missed a beat. An enviable pro.

About a month after shooting in New Mexico, I was called in to do some looping back in LA. (Looping is when a scene plays on repeat for a voice actor to match their dialogue for the episode.) As I was finishing up, who comes in but Carol Burnett? I made quick eye contact and was preparing to say a short but formal hello, when she chirped, "Hi, Jim!" Carol Burnett remembered my name. Put that on my headstone: CAROL BURNETT REMEMBERED MY NAME.

I haven't told you everything that happened after Nick's party where Mike had told us about our "final thirteen." A week or so later, during a private moment on set, Amy asked me if I knew what they'd planned for Jerry.

"Jerry?"

"Yeah," she whispered. "Jerry, Garry, Larry . . ."

"Oh! No," I sniffled. "What? What is it? What's going on?"

"Your character," Amy said, breaking into a grin, "is going to be mayor."

"What?!"

"Yeah! We're thinking about doing a jump into the future so the audience can see what our characters' lives are like, and Jerry is the mayor of Pawnee . . . the mayor! Forever!"

Either Amy had stopped whispering or my expression had given me away, but my mix of sad-happy tears had converted to happy-happy. I told myself that this storyline might only be what Amy was hearing at the time. Nothing was definite, which meant it could all change. Still, I so wanted it to be true.

Endings on TV shows rarely nail it, sorry to say. It's such a tough thing to do. How do you write one to a show that makes everyone happy? It seems an impossible feat. So many producers and writers are trying to please every viewer that you end up pleasing nobody. What did the singer Ricky Nelson say? "You see, you can't please everyone, so you got to please yourself." *Ew, Ricky!* But seriously, I can count on one hand the number of shows that nailed the ending. *Six Feet Under. M*A*S*H. The Sopranos.** *Mad Men.* So, going in, we knew the bar was high. We didn't let it affect us, though. The writers simply did their work, and we did ours.

Mike Schur

There are things when you look back at a show—I watch episodes with my kids now—and I'm like, Why did I cut that joke or why didn't I leave that? Why did I do that? I am still annoyed with myself a thousand times when I watch it. There are things about the finale that annoy me, too, just because I can't help it. What I like about it is that there was an element of the show that was essentially sort of wish fulfillment, I think, on the part of the creative team. The wish fulfillment was, What if there were a woman who was so dedicated to public service that she would sleep three hours a night, spend her own money, travel the world, and fight as hard as Leslie Knope fights to make the lives of the people in her town one percent better with whatever thing she had to do that week. In America in the twenty-first century, that is a very wish-fulfillment kind of an idea. What I do like about the finale is that the finale is essentially that wish

* IMHO.

fulfillment run amok, where you get to see everyone's future and you know that everyone turns out okay. Everyone is happy and everyone's life goes well. Jerry dies peacefully in his sleep at one hundred years old, surrounded by his family and holding his wife's hand, after being the mayor of the town for eighteen years or whatever. Retta finds an appropriately matched life partner for herself. Tom, who had always been a striver and had a million failures, learned how to turn his failures into a success. One after another, you just go down the line and you get to see the things that made all of the characters who they were play out in the future. It's a little bit sappy, could be one criticism. When I think about that and the truth of that, I am like, "Yeah, it fucking is; it's a little bit sappy. God damn right." I don't apologize for that.

When *Entertainment Weekly* decided to do a cover story on the cast to coincide with our final episode, I was reminded of the power of friendship.

Entertainment Weekly had always been kind to us throughout our run. They were kind in the lead-up to this finale story, too, enthusiastically relaying as much information as they could ahead of time. This would be a cover spot, they said, and get this: each actor will be getting their own spread within the magazine! The cover plus a special section? This was like a double shot of Jack Daniel's on the Fourth of July.

Then I got the call . . .

It was my publicist, Rob. "Jim, I have some bad news," he said. Rob is not an I-deliver-bad-news kind of guy. Even his bad news is tricked out to sound good, like a hologram of information. He's a pro at handling actor egos. "We got the official call, and it turns out that you and Retta will not be on the cover with the rest of the cast for *Entertainment Weekly*," he said.

What?! I flashed back to the pain of being excluded from the *People* shoot years ago. It made no sense. I'd been on *every single* episode of the show, a stat that few others could claim—which is not to say I was trying then or now to compare myself to my castmates. However, being left off the cover signaled that I'd never been seen as an official cast member. That wasn't only nonsensical. It was mean.

Rob tried to assuage me. "Just so you know," he said, "everyone has been involved in trying to rectify this decision. The producers and even the writer of the piece have tried to go to bat for you and Retta." *Entertainment Weekly*'s defense was that putting me and Retta on the cover would've made it too crowded. They assured us we'd be getting equal treatment within the magazine, however.

On the day the *Entertainment Weekly* crew came to the set to shoot, we all participated in interviews before their team started to set up for the *official* cover image. "Let's go to my trailer," I said to Retta as they prepared the equipment. "We don't need to be there for this." Maybe this was a childish response in retrospect, but I held two opposing ideas in my head at that moment: one was that I was happy for my castmates for being honored in this way, and the second was that I was sad for me and Retta. "I just can't be here," I added. "Not today."

We were stepping off set when we were stopped by Jean from the wardrobe department, who told us, "Your white shirts are in your trailer." Everyone was supposed to wear white for the cover shoot, though I was confused because "everyone" up till then did not include us.

"Sorry, Jean," I said, "but Retta and I aren't doing the cover."

"Yes you are," she said assuredly.

Aw, poor Jean. Does she not know? Do I have to engage in some awkward conversation where I tell her that we have not been asked to? Do I have to receive her pity in place of my own?

"Jean, we're not," I said, this time more directly.

She leaned in, and I glimpsed a couple tears in her eyes. "You and Retta are absolutely doing the cover." I was floored. "Your white shirts are in your trailers," she repeated.

I later learned what had happened. Amy Poehler, our resident hero and mama bear, was told about the cover shoot and who was going to be in it. The magazine told her the same story—that the cover would look too busy and that Jim and Retta would be featured in the interior. It was the best they could do. Or that's what they thought then. My understanding is that Amy told the magazine something along the lines of, "If Jim and Retta aren't on the cover, then I'm not on the cover. Your current plan? Not gonna work." And just like that, the decision was reversed. We appeared on that *Entertainment Weekly* cover the same way we'd appeared on- and off-screen for the last seven years: together, as one big crazy family.

The mild embarrassment that could've ensued had Jean been wrong about our inclusion reminds me of a moment I witnessed when guesting on *Norm*, Norm MacDonald's sitcom, years ago. As usual, the cast and guest stars showed up for work, which began with a table read of the episode. This was a multicamera show where there was a live audience, like doing a play each week. After the table read, we spent the day rehearsing, with the knowledge that by the next day, there would be new lines. You never commit early scripts to memory because they will change. The next day arrived, and I was sitting at a table having a bagel, looking over my new lines, and chatting with the cast and other guest stars. There was a new guy at the table who told us that he was playing a certain role. It was confusing because that role had been played by someone else the day before. They had fired one actor and hired another. That happens. The awkward part was that about ten minutes later, the original actor of the role strolled up to the table with his breakfast in tow. He sat down and started talking with all of us, and the confusion mounted. A few minutes later, someone approached the original actor and whispered something in his ear. He looked a bit surprised and got up. When he returned to the table, he grabbed his food and backpack. Nobody had the nerve to look him in the eyes. Apparently, nobody had called to tell him that he had been fired. Ah, Hollywood.

I've heard it said that if you haven't been fired from a show at least once, then you're doing something wrong. I never understood that saying and, fingers crossed, I have yet to be fired.

In some ways, being left off that cover shoot would've felt like a firing. And that is just one of a million reasons, big and small, that Amy Poehler is one of the kindest people on the face of the earth. She didn't have to do any of that. It wouldn't have mattered to her career one bit whether Retta and I made the cover, but it mattered to the culture she'd helped create, where the sum of the parts was more important than any one actor—no matter if you were Rob Lowe, Rashida Jones, or Amy herself.

Amy Poehler had taken a moral stand as well as a business one. It was one thing for her to say, "This is not how we do things at *Parks*," but it was another to imply that the decision on *EW*'s part was ethically shortsighted. That is what makes Amy great—she's not interested in doing what's right according to the script; she's willing to pivot and swerve and U-turn as needed. In fact, Retta told me that when we were filming a promotion for all of the NBC shows all those years before, one of the producers had made a comment while we were going through the hallway that the way the cameras were capturing me and Retta was "fine because you're not going to see Jim and Retta in the final cut anyway." It was Amy who, no surprise, stood up for us. "Why are they wasting their time here if you're not going to see them?" she asked the NBC producer. Her directness solved everything.

If you see the final *Entertainment Weekly* cover, with all of us clad in our starched white shirts, you will also notice that the top of my face is obscured by the "EN" of the word "Entertainment." I remember saying to myself at the time, "Wow, they didn't even have the decency to show my entire face?" Then it hit me. Designers don't do anything without intent. "Oh my God," I said to Retta, "it's a tribute to Jerry Gergich. Of course his face would be covered. It's Jerry that would be left out, not Jim. I love it!"

There were several Jerry fans who complained online about the magazine's design decision, but let's acknowledge it's so clever. As Amy joked to me after the fact, sometimes a little controversy goes a long way. "By the way," she said with a smile, "I think you got more attention than any of us."

That's a Wrap

No, not our final airdate but my final set call for the show. My final drive to stage 21 at the CBS Radford lot. My last time pulling into my parking spot. The last time I'd laugh my ass off with the hair, makeup, and camera crew. The last time I'd shoot the shit with this amazing cast. The last time we'd all work together—not that it ever felt like it. Work, I mean.

When I stepped into my trailer that morning, I found it strangely empty. It lacked the usual junk I'd kept there and was now filled with neatly wrapped gifts and notes from cast and crew. I immediately began reading a few and quickly realized that if I was going to get through this day without being a total blubbering mess (it turns out that was not possible), then I would have to finish them later. Luckily, I'd brought my own notes and gifts for them. If I was going to cry, then I'd make others cry, damn it.

I asked our base-camp production assistant to distribute my notes, each professing my gratitude to the people who'd had such a wonderful impact on my life during the run. I'm not just talking about the cast. The people behind the camera had become family, too, and I'm in contact with many of them today. I can't stress enough the importance of an amazing crew. I know that actors often get recognition because we're the ones in front of the cameras, the ones lucky enough to portray characters that hopefully people at home (you!) fall in love with. But none of it exists without a competent and collaborative crew. From the people working craft services (the folks who keep us fed) to the top of the executive producer ladder, everyone has an important part to play.

My understanding is that we retained 85 percent of our crew over our seven-year run. That's an incredible number in the cutthroat TV world. When it was announced that the show would be ending with a thirteen-episode order, I would've expected some of the crew to start looking for other series that were going to do a full twenty-two, for the sake of job security. That would have made sense. Rather than heading for greener pastures, 99 percent of them stayed. They wanted to see it through. That's a huge testament to the kind of atmosphere we had. To this day, nothing makes me happier than showing up on a new shoot and seeing some of the folks from *Parks* working there.

Chris Pratt has kindly told me that I'm a good gift-giver. I try to think of the person and come up with something that will be meaningful and lasting. Usually a note, something they can read again and again. Here's another note: I love you, Pratt!

The gifts I received from the cast and crew were as good as any I could've given.

The emotions on set were higher than the pile of notes in my dressing room. I know I wasn't the only one trying to keep it together. I also noticed that there were a lot more people hanging around than usual. So many people I'd never seen before. I later found out that the studio and network folks decided they wanted to be there for the final scenes. Some had invited their close friends and family as well. These weren't the people we'd typically see on set, but when the end is nearing, the whole town comes out to celebrate.

The celebrations had begun in earnest with, I believe, the penultimate episode, "Two Funerals," in which, for my part, I become mayor of Pawnee thanks to Ben Wyatt's generosity. The inauguration of Garry (formerly Jerry) is a wild affair, with Roman legionnaires carrying me in a litter, a chorus singing K-Ci and JoJo's "All My Life," fireworks, and a hot-air balloon—all most likely meant for the marriage proposal Tom intended to make.

This fanfare was in the script, but, as with many of our shooting days, I didn't realize how extravagant it would all be until I got there. In preparation for the scene prior, when Leslie and I are in the limousine, Amy and I decided we'd crack jokes because we wanted our characters to appear to be in the middle of one long laughing session (as it

Up, up, and away in my beautiful, big balloon.

appears in the final take). What I saw once I stepped out of the limo blew my mind, though. So much so that I forgot I was supposed to be laughing. I think now about the time my mom visited me on the set for the film *Harvey* and she cried, saying, "This is all for you?" I wish she had been at Jerry's inauguration, because I would've answered, "Yes, Mom."

"We're going to get you about ten feet in the air before we cut away," one of the producers told me between takes. Well, the next thing I know I'm twenty feet up and getting higher by the second. When you watch the episode, Jerry looks terrified as he's rising up in the balloon. That's what the script called for. But let me tell you . . . I was not acting.

Despite its gloomy-sounding title, "Two Funerals" was a laugh factory for me, but the series finale made me a crybaby once again. It's during one of the last scenes, where Garry is surrounded by blond bombshells (Christie Brinkley among them) before he passes away prior to his one hundredth birthday. The funniest part about this scene is that while Garry has been made to look old, Gayle has a nearly wrinkle-free face. I remember Christie coming up to me to show me the wrinkles they'd put near her eyes. I'd been in makeup for five hours to look a hundred years old, and Christie looked like she'd just stepped out of *Vogue*.

This scene depicted the end of the Gergiches on the show, and since I reasoned that I might never work with Christie again, I couldn't get through this scene without crying. I swear, we must've done fifteen takes, and on each one I couldn't hold back the tears. I was such a watery mess that at some point Dean Holland (one of our favorites) came up to me and very politely said, "Jim, I need to get one with you not crying." This made me chuckle, at least momentarily. "Dean," I said, "I promise you I'm trying not to. I just can't—" And then came those tears again, like a Jackson Browne song on repeat. I tried everything in my actor's playbook not to cry, including attempting to trick my brain into imagining the stupidest thing possible, like a dog on a pogo stick for instance, but nope. Still teary. She told me not to worry, that we'd get through this together and that it didn't matter how many takes it took, she'd be there to help me along. It turns out Christie's selflessness made me even more emotional—she'd officially become the living embodiment of Gayle Gergich. "I love you, Christie," I said, "but saying that totally didn't help." And then I cried and laughed through tears some more.

Though I made it through those million takes, I was reminded of when I first watched the episode of *All in the Family* where Meathead and Gloria pack up and move to California. To my young mind, it was one of the saddest fictional things I'd ever seen. Now here I was, part of a show where I'd fallen in love with the Gergich family, as annoyingly blond as they were, and the actors who played them. If they were gone, well then, so was Jerry. Or Garry, as he was called by this point.

So flash forward to November 21 and my final set call on "One Last Ride," where the finality was inescapable and the celebrations tinged with happy tears. When you're filming the last episode of a show, you have what you call a series wrap, basically an excuse to applaud each person, individually, after they deliver their final lines. *That's a series wrap on Amy Poehler! That's a series wrap on Nick Offerman!* Everyone on set claps and howls and yells the nicest things they can. If you're me, you cry. And I swear, I cried for every single person. Aziz? Gone. Retta? Good night, nurse! Amy? Fugghettaboutit. I even cried for myself—who does that? Retta once told me she can make herself cry on a dime, but that she likes to have that moment just for herself. I seem to have that moment in front of everybody else, on a quarter.

While I made a public performance of crying, Retta found time for herself in her trailer. Though we were extremely proud of and grateful for our time on the show, we both had anxiety about what would come next. Retta thought she could go back to stand-up at the very least, not that I think she exactly wanted to, while I suppose I could've lived for a while on the glory of *Parks*. Thing is, maybe I thought that Jerry was all I had, sweet punching bag that he was. I thought that a wrap signified the end of our reign together. Everyone had clapped for me, but would they ever clap for me again?

Actors are their own worst enemies. Not long ago, a fan approached me and told me they had loved me on *Criminal Minds*. Now, 90 percent of fan interactions I have are about Jerry and *Parks*. That's why I froze when she mentioned *Criminal Minds*.

"Ummmm . . ."

"You were so good on it," she repeated.

"I'm sorry," I said, "but I wasn't on that show. You must be thinking about somebody else."

"No, you were on it," she said assuredly. "Jim O'Heir, right?"

"Yes . . ."

"I loved you in that one episode!"

"But I wasn't on it!" I pleaded.

Then she did what every actor hates: she pulled out my IMDb page, which listed the episode name, year, etc. Not only was I in it, but the episode was the first part of the two-part series finale! The penultimate episode of an iconic series. Who the hell forgets that? All I can say in my defense is that I've got over two hundred IMDb credits and I'm getting old.

Thankfully, I am remembered as more than a big ol' pot of coffee, which is how I'm dressed in the last scene. The last scene in which we're together. How I wrapped my seven seasons on *Parks*. How I'm dressed as we're all saying our goodbyes. One

How appropriate . . . my last day on set and I'm dressed as a giant pot of coffee. A perfect Jerry moment.

giant pot of coffee. Tom says to me at the end of that scene, "You're the mayor, Garry! Have some dignity." And he's right. There's nothing dignified about a singing and dancing giant foam coffeepot.

Mike Schur

The show in its final hour made one last argument on behalf of love and friendship, kindness and optimism, and happiness. When you make an argument for those things, especially in the modern world, you are going to be accused of being a wallflower or naive or sappy or whatever. So be it. The message of the show that Amy and I used to talk about all the time was that optimism beats pessimism. As tempting as it is to give in to pessimism or denialism, and to throw up your hands and say, "None of this matters; it's all bullshit. The world is screwed up, we're all going to die, and climate change is going to ruin the planet." Yes, that is an option and if you do that, congratulations. Now what? Or you can be Leslie Knope and you can say, "I'm going to keep fighting. I don't know, maybe it won't work, but I'm going to keep fighting. I'm going to keep trying." And the finale sort of puts a fine point on that idea, which the show trafficked. And now, keep in mind that we did that entire show pre-Trump presidency, which was a key to us being able to actually play that idea out. I think if you did the show now, it would be very different. You wouldn't be able to make that argument because that argument seems even less likely or truthful or whatever. During the Obama years, that argument—that just plug away, plug away, plug away, do your job, try to do the right thing when you can, try to be a good friend, try to be a good spouse or daughter or father or whatever—that's a good idea for a show. In the way that TV shows talk to the audiences that watch them, I'm happy that that was the message that we tried to send.

Amy Poehler liked to articulate the idea that less is more. Better to leave the audience wanting more than to give them everything you think they need, she said. Dressing as a coffeepot was certainly giving them something, though I don't know what. But maybe I took Amy's wisdom to heart when, on the night of the airing of "One Last Ride," the cast and I took to the soundstage of *Late Night with Seth Meyers*. Seth was a big fan of the show, and a good friend of Amy's from their *SNL* days, and he had moderated panels with us in the past. Typically, when busy people like Seth host panels, they're asked if they'd like to be briefed with all kinds of questions and information about the show and its actors, but Seth would always decline because he knew the show as well as we did. Of course, it helped that he and Amy are dear friends. It never hurts to have a friend in Hollywood. So, when our pal Seth told us that he was going to host all of us on the night the final episode aired, we knew we had to up the stakes a bit.

Before flying us out, Seth's producers ran through the scheduled programming, which consisted of a Q & A and a game where we'd toast one another timed by a twenty-second clock. Oh, and as the credits rolled, they told us, we'd regale the audience with a sing-along of Mouse Rat's "5,000 Candles in the Wind," aka "Bye-Bye Li'l Sebastian," topped off by Pratt playing guitar. You can't get more perfect than that.

The convivial spirit was fired off before we even got on the soundstage. Mike Schur was there, as was Morgan Sackett, and though there was an understanding that this might be one of the last times we were all in a room together, it also felt like a throwback to the first time we came in for a table read. That was the magic integral to *Parks*—all for one and one for all. And we all felt magical that night.

Then it came time to do the show. One by one we were introduced to join Seth onstage—here's Amy Poehler, here's Nick Offerman, here's Mike Schur. (Yes, even Mike accompanied us on TV.) As it happened, I was seated on the far right of Seth (far left if you're watching the screen), and next to me was Adam Scott, and next to him, Aubrey Plaza.

For this hour-long special, we laughed and told stories, and I remember thinking that all the stories told the world over could never accurately communicate the love I have for those people. Still, we tried, and, dare I say, we did, because when it came time for Pratt to toast me, and for me to toast him, I was a blubbery mess. No surprise to you by now, I know, but all these years later, I'm struck by how affected I still am by them. Chris said, "You are so genuine, incredibly thoughtful, you're an amazing gift-giver, you're a great listener, you're a wonderful friend, and you're a great spokesman for our show. When people hit you up online you're always kind to them, and, you know what, and you're sensitive and don't let anyone ever make you feel bad about that. That's awesome."

It was like he'd written the summary of this book, and of my life. I returned the favor, saying, "Chris Pratt began in a pit, he was lying in a damn pit, but here's the thing—he was so loving, and such a great person then, he's now one of the biggest stars in the frickin' world and he's the same person he was in that pit. And I mean that with all the love, there's no one kinder and more gracious than Chris Pratt. I love him with all my heart."

But this likely isn't the part you remember, nor the part I intended to tell you about. It's merely background before the . . .

Okay, fine, I'll tell you.

When Seth went to his final commercial break before our last segment—the one where we were to break into song—I sat there trying to find some of my friends in the audience who had made the special trip to witness this important moment of my career. I was halfway between smiling to them and mouthing "Heyyyyy" when I received a tap on the arm. It was Aubrey Plaza, who had leaned over Adam Scott and was now whispering in my ear. "Do you want to make out during the credits?" she asked.

That was it. No preface, no irony, no bull crap. A totally straightforward Aubrey/April-like question. It took me all of two seconds to respond in a totally shit-scared-but-trying-to-be-cool Jim O'Heir way: "Uhhh . . . yes." I don't recall what was going through my mind, if anything was at all. I knew this: if Aubrey Plaza asks you to make out, then you make the heck out.

I just agreed to WHAT?!

The commercial break ended and Seth welcomed back the studio audience as well as the viewers at home. Pratt had been given a guitar and was now standing front of stage, ready to launch into song. Meanwhile, Seth chirped, "My thanks to Amy Poehler, Aziz Ansari, Nick Offerman, Jim O'Heir, Aubrey Plaza . . ." Councilman Jamm walked across the stage, feigning rudeness, as Pratt began strumming the chords to our favorite song, and then Aubrey leaned over . . .

Now, as you might recall, I didn't receive the best kissing advice of my life from my father or health ed teacher, but from the inimitable Rob Lowe, who told me—let me repeat his advice here—that "you keep your mouth closed when you go in for the kiss. When your lips meet, it's all up to your scene partner. If she parts her lips, then you can follow suit. If she slips in a little tongue, then you can go ahead and say hello with yours. Basically, it's whatever your scene partner is comfortable with."

Well, Aubrey had her tongue down my throat so fast that I had no choice but to "follow suit" and "say hello" with mine. If you watch the video, you'll notice that this is no ordinary kiss. No way. Aubrey and I are engaged in a full-blown make-out sesh, like a *Cruel Intentions* make-out. Or was it *The Shining*, with Jack Torrance kissing the beautiful woman who turns out to be the saggy old lady. (In this case, I'm the saggy old lady.) Either way, we were going at it.

The sacrifices I make for a laugh, let me tell you.

My favorite part about the "kiss," beyond the actual kiss of course, was the surprise and mortification on my friends' and castmates' faces. You can see Retta and Aziz open-mouthed and tapping each other in broad gestures of disbelief. Even better, Pratt had no idea any of this was going on because he was facing the audience and leading us in a triumphant rendition of Mouse Rat's song. You can hear the audience's laughter (and horror), so loud that the song is barely audible, and yet, Pratt is totally locked into it. As a true front man should be. He joked with me recently that Aubrey Plaza's life is like performance art. "I loved being part of that installation," he said of his time with her on the show.

Who would've known that one hour later, we'd be making out?

The performer-of-the-year award goes to none other than Ms. Plaza, who, yet again, proved how smart she is. You see, this bit wouldn't have worked if she'd decided to make out with Ben or Chris. It worked because she made out with Jerry, whom her character was always so dismissive of. It worked because she'd chosen the fattest and oldest guy on set. It worked because she pursued it with utmost conviction, in the only way Aubrey Plaza knows how.

To this day, I'm frequently asked about this decision, whose idea it was and how it happened. And I am proud to report that it was 100 percent not my idea—as if!—and that all credit goes to Aubrey's brilliance and devil-may-care spirit. What I can tell you is that when I'm asked what it was like to make out with Aubrey Plaza, my response is as follows: "There are winners and losers in life, and in this circumstance, I was most certainly at the winning end."

It's worth mentioning that when I talked to Retta years later and told her that I'd heard, after the fact, that Mike Schur was uncomfortable with Aubrey's choice, Retta, ever the truth-teller, told me, "Well yeah, so was I! Did you see my face?" Mike has since joked to me that Aubrey is an "agent of chaos," and I couldn't agree more.

A couple days after "the kiss," as I was planning to leave New York, who else was waiting outside the hotel but TMZ, who, until this point, had never cared about me. The only time they had before was to get closer to the show's principals, I later learned. Well, unlike that one time, I knew exactly what they were seeking as they stood outside my hotel—Aubrey and I were already the talk of the town, or at least the talk of the fan sites. "Jim O'Heir," came a voice, "what was it like kissing Aubrey Plaza?" And then another voice, this one more urgent: "Is Aubrey not in a relationship any longer?" This illogical line of reasoning was followed by a third: "Are you two in a relationship?"

Yeah, yeah, I thought, *Aubrey and I are getting hitched. We're getting married!*

Remembering my trusted publicist's advice when it came to the tabloids, I avoided these questions but did ask some TMZ reporters for recommendations on how to locate the closest subway. A side note: if you ever spot me walking around New York City, it's usually because I'm lost trying to find a train station. I've always had this fantasy of riding the New York City subway late into the night, but I've never fulfilled it. So, if you see me walking the big bad streets of New York, help a guy out!

Chris Pratt

I like when something ends on a high note. I don't like beating something into the ground for the sake of doing it. It's always bittersweet, the relationships you build with people, because they come to a close. It doesn't mean you'll never know those people again, but the nature of those relationships naturally changes—and, in my experience, it usually means you won't see them again. Years will pass, and that's the nature of this business. It's like a circus when they pull out the stakes and roll up the tents and the crew leaves town. Before all of that, you have this goal to make it real and it becomes real, and then . . . then it's over. And there's this sadness at the end of it, a bittersweetness. I've wrapped up several franchises at this point, and it's no different. Rarely does someone become your top-five that you're going to talk to every day. For the most part, you just go your separate ways, and that's just sad.

The sweetest thing happened the night of *Seth Meyers*. Following the extended make-out sesh, the cast attended a wrap party hosted by the show's producers. On the way out of 30 Rock and into our personal cars to get to the party, we were met by hundreds of screaming fans, which culminated in yet another one of my "Beatles moments." Although we were on a strict schedule, not to mention that security was adamant about our staying in queue and not being drawn by the adoration, I couldn't help myself. I leapt out of the line anyway, posed for selfies, and signed some ass cheeks.

The producers had rented a restaurant with an open bar with all the amenities. Tons of great food and the jittery mood of celebration. There was the entire cast plus some writers and several friends of the cast, including Rachel Dratch, a dear friend of Amy's—and the accompanying feeling that this could actually be the last event with all of us together in one room.

We didn't know then that we'd be invited to PaleyFest ten years later or that there'd be special reunion requests. And we didn't know then that *Parks* was the kind of show I'd be asked to write a book about or host a podcast on.

I couldn't have known any of that back then, so I took every minute of this party seriously. By which I mean I partied! Hard.

We also watched the finale for the first time, as a cast, together. We settled into seats as a TV was turned on and the opening credits rolled. To my knowledge, this was the first time any of us was seeing the finale, and only hours after it had aired. It's possible that Amy had seen it, or at least parts, but the child-like giggles I heard around me signaled that this was the first time for most of us.

The party continued late into the night, but at some point someone decided that it was getting late, which signaled to others that it was approaching "closing time." All good parties must come to an end, and this was that time—when several of the guests were seen saying their goodbyes and heading for the exits.

I didn't want to go out with a standard goodbye. None of us cast members did. That's when we found ourselves loitering by the staircase next to the door, like kids outside a 7-Eleven at 1 a.m. With nothing more to look forward to after this moment, and every indication that we were right where we needed to be.

Heck, for seven years, we felt we were always right where we needed to be.

I'm not sure who initiated the hug, but it spread among the cast like an adorable octopus. Once I saw its friendly tentacles approaching me, I received it in kind. Soon, it comprised the whole cast, and the whole cast comprised it. One big happy family hug.

I swear that that hug lasted a whole five minutes. Eight of us—the best of colleagues, many of us the best of friends—embracing the relationship we'd created. In relationships, you don't leave without hugging goodbye. You hug and you stay hugging for a minute, maybe several. In this case five. You say, "I love you." You say, "Thank you so much." You say, "I can't wait to see you again soon."

Our last location shoot. How fitting that it was in a park.

This was our "table read" for
the special episode we shot
during COVID.

A complete representation of solidarity.

Parks Special

Trying to "catch our dreams" in the recording studio with director Robert Weide (at center, holding Aubrey's shoulders) and members of Mouse Rat.

Acknowledgments

I'm grateful to so many amazing people who have had an impact on my life. To begin, John and Eileen O'Heir gave me a childhood filled with love, respect, and possibilities. They might not have understood my dreams, but they always supported them. I miss them every day. My siblings, John O'Heir, Beth O'Heir, and Ann O'Heir Blair, have always had my back. Life will always have its ups and downs, but having my brother and sisters in my corner brings me comfort and the knowledge that I'm never on my own. I was blessed with a family cushion. If all had failed, I would've still had a place where I would be welcome and loved. These siblings brought me the greatest nieces of all time: Emily Paganelli, Kristin Paganelli, Nicole Duncan Warke, and Hannah Duncan. They're smart and funny, and they put up with my ridiculousness. I love them all.

I come from a funny family. I mean really funny. There's nothing like a good belly laugh, the kind that takes your breath away. I want to thank my slew of aunts, uncles, and cousins who have kept me in stitches over the many, many years. Special shout-outs to my Aunt Pat, Aunt Mary, and Aunt Noonie. You all helped mold the person I've become. It's nice to know there's someone to blame. ;)

I want to thank my White Noise cast, whom I was with when this journey began in 1986: Patrick Cannon, Ned Crowley, Meg Moore Burns, Jeff Johnson, and Ruth Novak. We created shows that were original, crazy, and pretty damn smart. Patrick wrote *Stumpy's Gang*, the play that brought me to Los Angeles in 1994 and changed the course of my life forever. Without Patrick

I don't know if I would have ever ventured west. Ned wrote and directed the film *Middle Man*, which I starred in after *Parks and Rec*. He wrote that film with me in mind. How blessed am I? These boys are still my ride-or-dies.

To my *Parks* cast, Amy Poehler, Nick Offerman, Rashida Jones, Retta, Aubrey Plaza, Chris Pratt, Adam Scott, Aziz Ansari, and Rob Lowe: I can't imagine a better cast to have taken this ride with. I loved going to work with you every day. Though Jerry might have been the office punching bag, you always treated me with love and respect. See you on the text chain.

To the show creators, Greg Daniels and Mike Schur: Your brilliance shows in all you do. You've created TV that will stand the test of time. The day you decided to hire me marked the change in the trajectory of my career. I'm also so grateful that you were willing to take a walk down memory lane and help me out with interviews for this book. Thank you!

To the producers, writers, and crew of *Parks*: Your tireless work to make the show happen always blew my mind. There are so many puzzle pieces that have to come together, and you always made it seem so easy. Special shout-out to producer Morgan Sackett, who made the impossible possible. Always calm and cool even when tornadoes were swirling around him. I'm also grateful for his help with this book.

To my friend, writer, and cohost of the podcast *Parks and Recollection*, Greg Levine: Your memory of our seven seasons on the show is astounding. Thank you for taking the time to help me fill in the gaps. Your knowledge made all the difference.

To Allison Jones, casting director extraordinaire: Your push for me to be seen by Greg and Mike is why I could write this book. Thank you.

To Matthew Daddona: The only reason this book exists is because of your hard work and ability to keep me focused. Not an easy task. You're such a good writer and have become a good friend. I will miss our Zoom sessions. You took my stories and assembled them into a coherent book that I'm so proud of.

To my manager, Lynda Bensky: We've been together for almost thirty years. For some reason, you still look the same while I look like hell. Thank you for your loyalty and love. We've had a partnership that has stood the test of time. I know you always have my best interest at heart, and I'm forever grateful.

To my publicist, Robbie Greenwald at Rogers & Cowan: You let me hang on to your coattails as your career blossomed, and I know I can always look to you for advice and guidance. I'm thankful that you're part of my team.

To my theatrical agent, Tim Weissman at Buchwald: I've known you since you were an agent's assistant when I first moved to LA. Now you're a big shot, and I couldn't love it more. I especially love that you're MY big-shot agent.

To my commercial agent, Pat Brannon at BBR: I walked into your office on August 8, 1994, and never looked back. You took a chance on a no-name from Chicago, and for that I'm so thankful.

To friends Marcia Wilke, Mo Collins, Kyle Colerider-Krugh, and Bari Halle: Thank you for listening and helping.

To Barb Sinchak and Jean Palasz. Two women I've known forever who mean the world to me.

To my team at HarperCollins, Mauro DiPreta, Allie Johnston, Sarah Falter, Kelly Dasta, and Kelly Cronin, and to Kanika Vora at R&CPMK: Thank you for choosing to collaborate with me. I've learned so much from working with you. You made this book novice feel like it's possible.

Thank you, Matt Latimer and Dylan Colligan at Javelin Literary, for coming up with the concept for this book and reaching out to me. You've been wonderful collaborators from the very beginning.

To my poker pals, Jim Underdown, Rob Guillory, Doug Hart, and Patrick Cannon: I must include your names in the book because you guys have a lot of dirt on me.

And last, but far from least, to my BFF Steve Ferrarese: Everyone needs a Steve in their lives. Incredibly smart, kind, funny, and supportive. Thank you for being there for me at every turn. I hope you know that I will always be there to return the favor.